21st Century Malaysia

21st Century Malaysia

CHALLENGES AND STRATEGIES IN ATTAINING VISION 2020

Edited by
MICHAEL YEOH

ASEAN
ACADEMIC PRESS
London

21ST CENTURY MALAYSIA:
CHALLENGES AND STRATEGIES IN
ATTAINNING VISION 2020

Edited by Michael Yeoh

Published by
ASEAN ACADEMIC PRESS LTD
P.O. Box 13945, London E5 0XY
England, United Kingdom
Fax: (0208) 533-5856
Visit us at *www.aseanacademicpress.com*
e-mail: *aapub@attglobal.net*

British Library Cataloguing-in-Publication Data
A catalogue record for this book is available from the British Library
ISBN 1-901919-44-7

Printed and bound in Malaysia

Contents

INFORMATION AND COMMUNICATIONS TECHNOLOGY (ICT)

INDUSTRY

SOCIAL

FOREIGN PERSPECTIVE

Preface

MIRZAN MAHATHIR
PRESIDENT, ASIAN STRATEGY & LEADERSHIP INSTITUTE (ASLI)

Change is indeed the only proposition that endures in today's rapidly evolving world that is increasingly characterised by globalisation and liberalisation. The only certainty today is arguably uncertainty. In the midst of a plethora of sweeping developments and changes in the world, Malaysia as a nation, too, has undergone a myriad of changes—for the better.

Malaysia in the wake of the 21st century is no longer the same as Malaysia in the infancy stage of its nationhood. From the days when the nation was akin to an infant scurrying for development with an agricultural-based economy and developing political and social maturity, Malaysia has significantly transformed itself into a dynamic, rapidly-industrialising and harmonious developing nation. The Asian economic crisis at the close of the 20th century had further reshaped the nation. This is evident in the consolidation of the multi-racial Malaysian society to stand united in riding the economic storm, the Government's tireless efforts in strengthening the financial and corporate sectors, and the rebuilding of an economy so that it is more resilient to external shocks and challenges. Malaysia has indeed come a long way. It is fair to say that we are now stronger than before.

But the road to mature nationhood is a long and winding one, at times an arduous one as well. Malaysia in the dawn of the 21st century is facing challenges greater than the nation has ever faced since its birth some 40 years ago. It is therefore pivotal for the nation to embark on far-sighted strategic thinking and planning, determined leadership and the search for innovative solutions to age-old problems. Malaysia has to constantly reinvent itself to stand up against the challenges of globalisation, liberalisation and the blurring of boundaries in this new era.

A myriad of new developments have taken place since our last similar publication, *Malaysia Today*, in 1997. The advent of information and communications technology, corporate restructuring, a host of landmark infrastructure projects and Malaysia's greater role in international relations are but just a few of the developments that have shaped Malaysia in these few short years and that are continuing to shape the nation in the 21st century.

The Asian Strategy & Leadership Institute therefore decided to undertake a publication which taps into the minds of those who are directly involved in formulating or implementing policies that will shape the nation in this new century and those charting the growth of the corporate sector. Their thoughts, insights and analyses on the nation's outlook in the 21st century and the challenges that lie ahead shed light on the way forward for Malaysia. Their articles also bring to light the many strategic initiatives by the Government as well as the corporate sector that have in one way or another contributed to our nation-building efforts. We are indeed deeply grateful to our distinguished and respected authors for their time and effort in producing articles of such outstanding quality and profound insight.

We also wish to express our heartfelt appreciation to our numerous contributors and sponsors. It is our earnest and fervent hope that this publication will achieve its main purpose of providing the reader with a better, wider and deeper understanding of Malaysia and the host of initiatives geared towards propelling the nation to greater heights in the 21st century.

Foreword I

MAHATHIR MOHAMAD
PRIME MINISTER OF MALAYSIA

This book, *21st Century Malaysia*, is undoubtedly a highly commendable publication by the Asian Strategy & Leadership Institute (ASLI). I wish to congratulate ASLI for initiating and undertaking this publication which provides profound insights into Malaysia at the dawn of the 21st century and the nation's future direction.

Malaysia has come a long way from our colonial roots that saw the land languishing in the economic backwaters upon independence in 1957. The young nation had to learn how it was to strive to build a nation that could stand tall in the world community. Today, at the dawn of the 21st century, Malaysia has indeed carved a name for itself among the peoples and nations of the world.

Nevertheless, there are still many challenges the nation will have to face as this new century is arguably different from the previous one. The wave of globalisation, the liberalisation of markets and industries, the advent of information and communications technologies, the new paradigm of knowledge economy, and the maturing society in terms of political and social sophistication present opportunities as well as challenges for the nation. Malaysia cannot be complacent. The Government has formulated policies and programmes to achieve Vision 2020. It is now up to all Malaysians to work hard to benefit from the opportunities available.

The compilation of articles in *21st Century Malaysia* provides an excellent overview of the nation's outlook in the 21st century, the many challenges the nation will have to embrace, the Government's strategies to propel the nation forward, and the private sector's initiatives and efforts towards realising common goals.

This publication will certainly serve as a useful reference and excellent guide for investors, corporate leaders, researchers and all those who wish to know more about Malaysia in the 21st century.

Foreword II

ABDULLAH AHMAD BADAWI
DEPUTY PRIME MINISTER OF MALAYSIA

These are the days of reckoning. Never before has Malaysia encountered the host of endless challenges at the dawn of this new century. Malaysia's transformation from an obscure nation to a rapidly-industrialising nation that thrives on national unity, racial harmony, economic aspirations, political maturity and social prosperity is indeed remarkable.

It is refreshing to see that there is a publication that provides a one-stop reference into the state of the Malaysian nation at the early rays of dawn in the 21st century and the pathways we shall tread from here.

I congratulate the Asian Strategy & Leadership Institute (ASLI) for conceptualising the idea of this highly useful and strategic publication, and successfully producing it for the honour of the nation.

Finance & Economy

Economy

Sustainability of Malaysia's Economic Recovery

Tun Daim Zainuddin
Former Minister of Finance

Malaysia has emerged from a deep financial and economic crisis that was, in several respects, even more serious than the economic recession of 1985. The crisis, which began as a localised currency devaluation, rapidly transformed into a crisis of regional proportions, reflecting in part the serious weaknesses of the international financial system as it did not provide protection for the economies of developing countries. This crisis was also a manifestation of the darker side of globalisation, especially in the liberalisation of the capital account of the balance of payments.

Given the gravity of the crisis in mid-1998 and continuing uncertainties, the Government was left with little choice but to take bold steps to curb the rapid decline not only of financial markets but activities in the real economy. These included the pegging of the ringgit and the implementation of selective capital controls. The latter, which attracted wide international interest, has since been gradually liberalised in line with improvements in the overall economy.

Consequent upon the various recovery measures, including measures to restructure and consolidate the financial and corporate sectors and the support provided by the encouraging external environment, the economy recovered and expanded by 5.8% in 1999 after experiencing a contraction of 7.4% in 1998. As economic activity continues to recover to pre-crisis levels, growth in Gross Domestic Product (GDP) increased by 8.5% in 2000.

The economic recovery has been particularly meaningful for Malaysia as we have managed to successfully mitigate both the social and economic costs of the crisis. Social stability and national unity were preserved during the crisis and economic costs were much lower than earlier anticipated.

The Government, through the National Economic Action Council (NEAC), has and continues to monitor closely developments in the economy. We recognise that economic recovery is a process that needs to be constantly appraised and adjusted to ensure that the progress we have achieved thus far continues. All sectors of the economy must, therefore, continue to be vigilant to current developments to ensure that the recovery is sustainable. We have to work persistently to ensure that no interruptions occur in the growth momentum and the economy returns to a path of sustainable growth.

While we are encouraged by the progress achieved in the consolidation of the financial sector and improving financial indicators, including lower short-term external debt relative to our reserves, compared to our neighbours, there still remains several policy areas that need further attention. One of the tasks ahead is in the area of corporate restructuring. The pace of corporate restructuring must continue to be maintained. The current improvements in the real economy should not lull corporations into complacency in regard to corporate management and financial restructuring. The corporate sector should instead utilise the current economic environment to address their internal problems as fast as possible to avoid more difficult adjustments later should the international and domestic environment turn less favourable in the future, given the uncertainties prevailing in the international environment.

The public sector will also need to be committed to speedy implementation of projects that have been planned and ensure that shortfalls in development expenditure are minimised. Not only are the expenditures important in promoting aggregate demand, they are also essential to expediting social capital formation. Although we have observed improvements in the implementation rate in the post-crisis period, there are still delays in the implementation process. Given the need to sustain the growth process, increasing the efficiency and responsiveness of the administrative machinery will continue to be a priority.

In order to ensure the return to more sustainable economic growth in the medium and longer term, the Government has initiated a number of studies, the findings of which will provide the basis for policy formulation. These include the Financial Sector Master Plan, the Capital Market Master Plan and the K-economy Master Plan. The financial and capital markets studies are important to the further development of the financial sector, in particular the banking sector and the capital market, given the need for the mobilisation of greater financial resources to facilitate the growth process. In the move to ensure that we keep abreast of the latest developments in the world economy as well as to enhance the nation's competitiveness and identify new sources of growth, the K-economy Master Plan outlines strategies for the greater infusion of knowledge in economic activities and identifies new sources of growth in knowledge-based activities for the future.

It was against this backdrop that Budget 2001 was drafted. The Budget aims to sustain economic recovery, promote wider use of information and communications technology (ICT) to address the issue of digital divide and promote new sources of growth, thereby ensuring the sustainability of long-term growth and the overall quality of life. It is my hope that the private sector responds positively to the new policy initiatives to ensure the attainment of sustainable economic growth in the post-crisis period instead of harping on the lack of support in regard to profit-making opportunities through the stock market.

The uncertain world economic environment and volatility of currency markets in the recent past has taught us to be pragmatic in addressing economic problems in the context of our economy. Whilst the free market regime theoretically promises much during normal times, it does not protect our interests and gives us little room to defend ourselves in times of crisis, as was evident in the events occurring during 1998. The management of the international economy remains inequitable and not much has changed since mid-1998, despite the rhetoric. The possibility of a new financial architecture evolving in the next few years remains, at best, remote.

Given these circumstances, our freedom to be pragmatic including making the appropriate domestic policy changes and adjustments remains a priority for us. In the meantime, we will continue to focus on policies to ensure our macroeconomic resilience and enhance our international competitiveness, thereby ensuring sustainable economic growth in the medium and long-term.

Fighting Back
The Story of the Malaysian Economy

Dato' Iskandar Dzakurnain Badarudin
Director-General
Economic Planning Unit, Prime Minister's Department

The attainment of Independence more than forty years ago heralded the beginning of development efforts to give the people a constantly improving quality of life. We chose to premise our development policy on the basis of free enterprise with the active involvement of the public sector. The development policy since 1970 has emphasised growth with considerations for equity. Strategies have thus been formulated with economic and social targets. This approach, together with the pragmatic and constant fine-tuning of policy, has resulted in the economy's impressive performance. Between 1970 and 1990, which coincided with the duration of the New Economic Policy (NEP), sound economic fundamentals enabled the economy to achieve real gross domestic product (GDP) growth of 6.7% per annum. At the same time, the incidence of poverty, as well as the inequalities in income, employment and ownership among the various ethnic groups, was considerably reduced. This contributed towards strengthening national unity.

The National Development Policy, 1991-2000, while maintaining the basic strategies of the NEP, emphasised the eradication of hardcore poverty and focused on human resource development and the creation of a commercial and industrial Bumiputra community. During the period of 1991-97, the economy grew rapidly at 9.2% per annum, exceeding the growth achieved over the previous two decades. This growth was accompanied by low rates of inflation, rising per capita income and a reduction in the incidence of poverty, thus raising the living standards of all Malaysians.

THE FINANCIAL CRISIS

However, in mid-1997, Malaysia was affected by the financial crisis that was triggered initially by the speculative attack on the Thai baht. This led to a deterioration in market sentiments and an erosion in investor confidence, which in turn resulted in the massive outflow of short-term capital, the drastic decline in the value of the ringgit and the fall in the stock market. Despite the adverse effects on sections of society, Malaysia successfully avoided the extreme effects experienced by some regional economies, such as high unemployment, mass poverty, massive bankruptcies and civil unrest. This was made possible by strong initial conditions, both in terms of the real economy and the financial sector, as well as the swift, pragmatic and innovative measures introduced by the Government.

Malaysia introduced a series of policy packages to deal with the crisis. At the initial stage, the Government adopted measures that included many features of the International Monetary Fund's prescription for the recovery of the economies of the region. Fiscal expenditure was reduced by 20% and monetary policy was tightened. While these measures were able to moderate inflation and reverse the deficit in the current account of the balance of payments, they caused severe liquidity problems and a drastic fall in domestic demand. This led to the rapid contraction of the economy.

When it became evident that these measures did not result in the expected economic recovery, the Government decided to chart its own course of action. It set up the National Economic Action Council tasked with the responsibility of preparing the National Economic Recovery Plan.

The Plan contained recommendations to stabilise the currency, restore market confidence, maintain financial market stability, improve economic fundamentals and address the equity and socioeconomic agenda. Among others, the Government reversed the policy of reducing public expenditure by introducing a stimulus package of RM7 billion, and eased monetary policy by gradually reducing Bank Negara Malaysia's intervention rate from 11% to 6% and lowering the statutory reserve requirement from 13.5% to 4% in stages. To strengthen the resilience of the financial sector, the Government established Danaharta, the national asset management company, to address the rising non-performing loans in the portfolios of the banking sector; Danamodal to recapitalise and consolidate the banking sector and the Corporate Debt Restructuring Committee to facilitate the voluntary debt restructuring of viable companies.

Selective capital control measures were adopted as pre-emptive measures on September 1, 1998 to regain monetary independence and insulate the economy from external currency turbulence.

The ringgit was also pegged at RM3.80 to the US dollar. A 12-month holding period was imposed for foreign portfolio investment to deter the movement of short-term capital so as to avoid excessive volatility in domestic financial markets. This condition was relaxed later with the adoption of the repatriation levy following improvements in the domestic economy.

The policies adopted by the Government enabled the rapid recovery of the economy. The economy rebounded from a contraction of 7.4% in 1998 to record a strong growth of 5.8% in

1999 and 8.5% in 2000. The accompanying low inflation rate, strong trade surpluses and improved reserves reflect the fundamental strength and resilience of the economy.

Moving Ahead

While Malaysia has come out of the crisis and is strongly on the path of steady growth, it faces new challenges. The rapid advancements in information and communications technology and accompanying globalisation are fast changing the basis of competitiveness. A country's competitiveness is no longer dependent on the traditional factors of production such as land and labour, but rather the capacity to acquire and utilise knowledge.

Knowledge Economy

After the successful transformation from an agricultural to an industrial economy over the last three decades, Malaysia is now developing its capabilities and capacities to move into the knowledge economy (K-economy). This is best demonstrated by the Government's initiative to develop the Multimedia Super Corridor (MSC) as a world-class IT hub for the introduction and synergistic expansion of IT-related and multimedia industries. The development of the MSC and its attractiveness, particularly in terms of the state-of-the-art infrastructure and the package of fiscal and non-fiscal incentives offered, are testimony of the nation's commitment to develop its IT capabilities.

In moving towards a K-economy, Malaysia is also committed to establishing itself as the regional centre of excellence in areas such as IT, financial services, insurance, transport and communication, travel and tourism, health and education. In this regard, aggressive efforts will be taken to develop the prerequisites of a K-economy—adequate supply of skilled manpower, a strong base in Science & Technology and R&D, and the necessary infrastructure.

The K-economy is also expected to open up new opportunities in the manufacturing sector, particularly in areas where there is scope for innovation and enhancement in technology. This will contribute towards the structural transformation of the economy, raise income levels and increase opportunities for all.

Promoting Investment

Malaysia will also continue to welcome foreign direct investment (FDI) as it has brought benefits in terms of the transfer of technology and managerial expertise, employment creation, new product development, trade generation and access to new markets. In addition, FDI is an important source of capital. Malaysia will continue to provide a liberal and competitive environment for investors by ensuring the provision of suitable supporting infrastructure; making well-trained manpower available, ensuring consistency of policy, unhindered repatriation of profits and expeditious approvals for investments; and the provision of attractive incentive packages. Domestic investment will be encouraged to further develop indigenous capability. Efforts will also be taken to promote complementarity between domestic and foreign investment.

Conclusion

As a small open economy, Malaysia is committed to a progrowth and business-friendly policy and will ensure that its development strategy continues to be private sector-driven. This liberal trading regime, which has been Malaysia's hallmark as a trading nation, will be pursued vigorously while we seek to become a developed nation in our own mould in the next two decades, as envisioned in Vision 2020.

The Malaysian Experience

Restructuring and Recovery of Non-Performing Loans

Dato' Azman Yahya
Chairman, Pengurusan Danaharta Nasional Bhd

Malaysia's approach in protecting the integrity and stability of the financial sector during the economic crisis of 1997/98 has been swift, comprehensive and effective. In this endeavour, importance was placed on being pre-emptive which ensured the continued functioning of the financial sector. In fact, one can attribute the continued functioning of the financial sector as one of the reasons for the quick turnaround in the Malaysian economy.

POSITION OF STRENGTH

It is worth highlighting that Malaysia actually entered the economic crisis from a position of strength. For instance, the risk-weighted capital ratio (RWCR) of the banking system as at end June 1997 was a comfortable 12%, way above the minimum requirement of 8%, while the net non-performing loan (NPL) ratio was only

2.2%. That was an important factor as it helped shape the policy approaches that the country adopted in reviving the economy.

In managing the economic crisis, Malaysia also enjoyed several key favourable factors that provided the country with greater flexibility in policy responses. These included a significant improvement in the external balance, low external debt, the containment of inflation, a high savings rate, a relatively low employment rate and a functioning banking system.

As a pre-emptive measure to protect against systemic risks in the financial sector, three special purpose vehicles were set up, i.e. Danamodal to recapitalise ailing banks, Danaharta to address the non-performing loan problems of financial institutions and the Corporate Debt Restructuring Committee (CDRC) as an arbitrator of corporate debt resolutions. Together with Bank Negara Malaysia, the institutions played complementary roles within the overall financial restructuring efforts.

THE EARLY PERIOD

During the period of turmoil, uncertainty prevailed in many quarters of the economy. There were criticisms from both the domestic and international community in terms of governance, transparency and independence of Malaysian institutions and companies.

When the Government's mandate came for the set-up of the special purpose vehicle to address the problem of non-performing loans (NPLs) in the banking system, we immediately identified the need to tackle perception issues and criticisms with regard to the transparency and independence of the Government. We knew all eyes were on us, so tread carefully we did. We had to be clear on the institution's role and objectives from the outset, so that a strong foundation could be built to support growth for the structure and operating perimeters.

Crossroads

Foremost on our minds were the products that we were grappling with, NPLs and the sensitivities surrounding the issue. Early criticism from various quarters even before Danaharta was incorporated was that Danaharta was being set up as a bail-out vehicle for certain individuals or groups caught in the financial mire of the day. Were we to become a bad bank then, where all the bad loans would be parked, stored and forgotten? We were met with scepticism in all aspects; our *raison d'être*, our effectiveness, our independence and our resources.

All the criticisms turned out to be constructive as it focused on the weaknesses that could turn out to be our 'Achilles heel', thus paving the road to be taken. It became clear that Danaharta had to be established as an independent institution that could quickly and effectively act upon its objectives with a fair amount of market-driven efficiency, while keeping in mind the concerns of national economic recovery and the interests of the nation as a whole.

The Road Taken

To establish Danaharta's framework, we undertook a preliminary study of asset management companies around the world, including the Resolution Trust Company set up in the United States and Securum in Sweden.

In a continuum of these institutions, one can find the rapid disposition asset management institutions at one end and the warehousing type at the other. In the middle are what we call true asset management institutions that are more market-driven in dealing with NPLs.

Danaharta took the middle road of becoming a true asset management company, wholly owned by the Government and regulated by the institutional and market laws of the land, yet given specially designed faculties to carry out its objectives with speed and efficiency. It also emphasised on matters of disclosure and transparency and steered by a clear governance structure and market-driven considerations.

Pengurusan Danaharta Nasional Bhd was incorporated on July 20, 1998 as a wholly Government-owned asset management company regulated by the Companies Act 1965 and the Banking and Financial Institution Act 1989 with very focused objectives. First, it acquires NPLs from financial institutions, thus allowing them to focus their attention on their core business activity which is to lend to viable borrowers. Second, Danaharta has to optimise the recovery value of the acquired assets. In carrying out its objectives, the Pengurusan Danaharta Nasional Bhd Act 1998 was passed, outlining Danaharta's framework and existence as well as conferring special powers of acquisition and disposal of assets.

PENGURUSAN DANAHARTA NASIONAL BHD ACT 1998

The Danaharta Act, which became effective on September 1, 1998, provides the legislative framework for Danaharta to undertake its unique mission and ensures that Danaharta is able to execute its job in an efficient and economic manner. This is important because the quicker Danaharta can complete its special mission, the greater will be the benefits to the economy and taxpayers.

SPECIAL POWERS

The Act's main thrust is based on two principles. Firstly, the ability to acquire NPLs with certainty of title. Secondly, the ability to manage the assets or collateral acquired for loans that cannot be restructured in two ways:

- Appointing Special Administrators to manage the affairs of distressed companies, and

- Providing an efficient foreclosure process for the sale of the underlying collateral.

The appointment and termination of these Special Administrators are governed by the Oversight Committee. Danaharta's ability to foreclose on property assets and sell the assets efficiently, bypassing the court auction process, is provided by an amendment to the National Land Code.

Governance and Control

Given these strong powers, it was important to establish a clear governance structure that would facilitate its use effectively and in a transparent manner. Realising this, the following governance and control structure was established.

Steering Committee

The activities of all the three sister agencies are coordinated through a Steering Committee chaired by the Central Bank Governor. The Steering Committee oversees and monitors the policies, operations and progress of the three agencies to ensure that they operate in a structured and cohesive manner.

Oversight Committee

One of the milestones featured in the Pengurusan Danaharta Nasional Bhd Act 1998, which facilitated debt resolution or restructuring, was the introduction of Special Administrators whose role and scope of work are similar to those of the Administrators in Australia and Chapter 11 resolution in the US.

In relation to this, Section 22 of the Pengurusan Danaharta Nasional Act 1998 provides for the establishment of an Oversight Committee. Where a borrower is a company, Danaharta has the right to appoint Special Administrators over the corporate borrower or the security provider if the corporate borrower is unable to pay its debts or fulfil its obligations.

In addition, Danaharta must be satisfied that the appointment would optimise value or is in the public interest.

Before a Special Administrator can be appointed or terminated, Danaharta must seek prior approval from an Oversight Committee formed for this purpose. The Oversight Committee comprises three members, one each from the Ministry of Finance, Securities Commission and Bank Negara Malaysia.

Board of Directors

The Board of Directors is the focal point of Danaharta's governance structure. It supervises all activities and maintains control through executive and non-executive committees, including the Board Executive Committee, Audit Committee and Remuneration Committee.

In achieving its objectives, Danaharta sought to incorporate international best practices in its operations with a unique fit to the requirements of its stakeholders and the Malaysian business environment.

A balanced approach was the key and this was reflected in the composition of its Board of Directors.

Internal Audit

An essential component of Danaharta's corporate governance structure is the Internal Audit and Compliance division. The division assists the Board of Directors, the Audit Committee and the management in achieving sound managerial review and control over all of Danaharta's activities to ensure that these can be carried out effectively and efficiently. This is achieved through an independent review of the fit for purpose of Danaharta's business controls and recommendations for improvements to ensure the control frameworks remain complete, effective and efficient. The division's role in this regard is to safeguard Danaharta's reputation by monitoring matters of independence and conflicts of interest as well as activities which Danaharta may not want to be associated with.

Voluntary and Mandatory Governance

Danaharta maintains a high standard of business conduct (based on international best practices) by setting out in the Standards of Business Conduct document, the general principles which govern Danaharta's activities and also the code of conduct for directors and employees in the performance of their day-to-day activities.

Transparency and Communications

We believe that one of the most effective methods of good governance is to be transparent—it not only disciplines the organisation to adopt best practices and sound governance, it is also seen to have these qualities. This is important for market confidence. Danaharta takes a proactive approach towards disclosure and communication, with ongoing communication lines available at Danaharta in the form of regular publications, operational reports, frequent media and analyst updates, e.g. press releases, parliamentary replies, annual reports/special reports and an active website.

Organisational and Human Resource Structure

Once the governance structure was in place, the next challenge was setting up Danaharta's organisational and human resource structure. Resources were scarce, but time was of the essence. We had to be up and ready for the first phase of operations by the end of the third quarter of 1998, just within three months of our incorporation. Our founding team members, mainly professionals from the merchant banking community, were already setting the pace and working around the clock to complete the operational infrastructure. Given our specific objectives and limited timeframe, Danaharta was moulded into a project organisation, with a flat but flexible organisational structure.

Operational Perimeters

As Danaharta delved into the acquisition phase, its operational perimeters began to take shape. Targets were set and to facilitate a transparent acquisition process, an asset acquisition guideline and a framework for valuation methodology were published. A key principle is the adoption of a market-driven approach. Danaharta operates along commercial principles, despite the fact that it is a Government-owned entity.

As the situation in Malaysia is not severely critical, Danaharta can afford to adopt a market-driven approach, and hence, it has no compulsory powers of acquisition. This means that transactions between Danaharta and the banks are done on a willing buyer-willing seller basis.

Danaharta's focus was on a system-wide carve-out of NPLs from the banking system so as to reduce the NPL ratio of the system to a tolerable level. In addition, to provide an incentive for the financial institutions to sell, any recovery by Danaharta over and above our cost will be shared on an 80(FI):20(Danaharta) basis.

Payment of NPLs

The financial institutions receive Danaharta bonds in payment for any purchase of NPLs. The bonds are government-guaranteed (thus zero risk-weighted), zero coupon, with a tenor of up to 10 years. They are priced against Malaysian Government Securities of similar tenor and are tradeable. The bonds provide the financial institutions with income (on an accretion basis), will improve their Capital Adequacy Ratio (the fuel indicator for financial institutions) and, being tradeable, can provide liquidity to those institutions that need it.

Having carved out the NPLs, what do we do with them?

Management of NPLs

As a true asset management company, Danaharta is involved in three phases of operations—the acquisition, management and subsequent disposal of the assets. Danaharta intends to add as much value to any asset as possible to optimise its recovery value.

This means that Danaharta is actively involved in the management of the asset and is not constrained by a too rigid timeframe, for instance, 5 to 7 years, although we are cognisant of the fact that the assets, once restructured or rehabilitated, must be disposed of to the marketplace as soon as possible. We must constantly be on our toes as it is easy to fall into the 'warehouse' trap and avoid organisational moral hazards with regard to the perpetuity of the institution.

Different countries around the Asian region such as Indonesia, Thailand, Korea and Malaysia take different approaches to asset management, reflecting the diversity of problems in these countries.

For instance, in Thailand where bankruptcy and foreclosure laws are relatively weaker, it made sense for them to dispose of the assets via auction in a rapid manner simply due to the sheer size of the loans portfolio in terms of the number of accounts. This is especially so since small loans including hire purchase contracts and residential mortgages form a significant amount of the assets, and it would have been administratively difficult to manage such assets.

KAMCO, the Korean asset management company, which in the past has taken a predominantly rapid disposition approach is, to a certain extent, thinking of managing the non-performing assets, although their problems are more manufacturing-inclined rather than property-related as is the case in Malaysia.

In Indonesia, where the banking system structure is fragile, an all-encompassing agency such as the IBRA (Indonesian Bank

Restructuring Agency) is needed to facilitate and implement the restructuring process.

No two asset management companies are, and can be alike, due to the different circumstances and legal framework which exist in each country. A comparison to determine which approach is best would be an exercise in futility, but it is useful to note the different approaches each country takes and draw out lessons to be learnt from their experiences. As for us, Danaharta has always been in constant touch with other regional asset management companies, exchanging views and sharing experiences. The prospects of bilateral and regional cooperation with other regional asset management companies are strong where a mutual sharing of resources and joint initiatives, especially in marketing, are in the pipeline.

Where are we two years down the road since our establishment in 1998?

Danaharta's Progress

As at September 30, 2000, we have carved out a total of RM46.78 billion (in gross value) of NPLs. The acquired NPLs of RM20.51 billion (to be distinguished from the NPLs under management) were purchased at an average discount of 55%. Danaharta has within its portfolio 3,177 accounts.

Out of the RM46.78 billion in our portfolio, we have restructured about RM35.28 billion, giving us an average recovery rate of 74% using various restructuring methods from settlement to plain loan restructuring and foreclosures.

Danamodal and CDRC's Progress

Danamodal, which is responsible for recapitalising 10 banking institutions during the crisis, has received early full repayment from five of these institutions, reflecting the better economic conditions.

As at July 2000, the CDRC has successfully completed 27 cases involving RM23.6 billion. These are in various stages of implementation. Presently, 22 cases involving a sum of RM16.7 billion are being worked out.

The progress we have achieved in accelerating financial and corporate restructuring has been good. We have progressively set new standards in corporate and debt restructuring. Our banks are stronger with NPLs moderating to 6.9% in July 2000 (six months classification), down from a peak of 11.4% in September 1998. The risk-weighted capital ratio has also improved from 11.8% at the end of 1998 (low of 9.9% at end-September 1998) to 12.8% in July 2000, significantly higher than the Basle standard of 8%. Meanwhile, the asset markets have also improved with the return of consumer confidence.

Prospects

Danaharta is but one of the measures that have been taken in response to the economic crisis. Together with Danamodal and the CDRC, we tackled the banking sector problems in the bud. Concurrently, Bank Negara Malaysia (BNM), introduced the Banking Sector Master Plan that would change the entire banking sector landscape in preparation for a more global open economy. The banking sector should basically become an engine of growth in its own right whilst supporting economic development.

At the same time, we should continue to pursue our long-term agenda of building a resilient, competitive and dynamic financial sector that is able to withstand negative impacts, meet the changing needs of its environment and provide a catalytic role in the sustained recovery and continued progress of the Malaysian economy.

Kuala Lumpur Stock Exchange

Ensuring Competitiveness in the New Millennium

Dato' Mohd Azlan Hashim
Executive Chairman, Kuala Lumpur Stock Exchange

Amongst the many challenges of the new millennium is globalisation—globalisation in standards, regulations and market practices. Rising to meet this challenge, the Kuala Lumpur Stock Exchange (KLSE) has formulated and implemented measures to ensure the continued competitiveness of the Malaysian market. With the objective of enhancing the rules and regulations, infrastructure development and the optimum use of resources—these measures are aimed at encouraging market participation in making the KLSE the investment destination of choice for all investors.

ENHANCING RULES AND REGULATIONS

In enhancing rules and regulations, the KLSE is introducing and implementing Disclosure Based Regulation (DBR), aimed at further updating and strengthening the KLSE's regulatory framework. DBR for companies listed on the exchange will ensure that standards of corporate disclosure adopted by the KLSE are in line with international requirements. DBR is set to facilitate the process of raising capital without compromising investor protection. In implementing DBR for the offer and issuance of securities, the KLSE will fully consider industry readiness and market requirements.

DBR is complemented by other initiatives such as enhanced disclosure guidelines, higher standards of corporate governance and the adoption and practice of international accounting practices which form a major part of the new Listing Requirements.

The recently launched new Listing Requirements for the KLSE, to an extent, reflect the future direction of the KLSE's regulations towards DBR. The KLSE's new Listing Requirements, introduced in January 2001, emphasise high standards of corporate governance that must be adopted and practised by Malaysian listed companies and greater enforcement in the regulation of listed companies.

Supervision standards of stockbroking companies have also been enhanced through the implementation of the Capital Adequacy Regulation (CAR) system. CAR is expected to minimise risk and regulate risk exposure to ensure the continued financial strength and prudential compliance of intermediaries participating in the securities industry.

Other measures introduced to complement CAR and strengthen intermediary supervision include requiring stockbroking companies to appoint compliance officers, increasing the frequency in the inspection of member companies and improving the online content of intermediary supervision through technological improvements to systems.

Encouraging Market Participation

Key to encouraging market participation is for the KLSE to continue promoting measures in enhancing cost competitiveness and accessibility of the Malaysian securities market. The reduction in transaction costs is part of these measures.

Whilst the move to reduce transaction costs is driven by the need to make the Malaysian securities market more competitive, the move also provides the right impetus to enhance the use of technology in industry operations and processes.

Reduced transaction costs will also encourage improvement in market liquidity. The reduction was implemented in two stages, the first stage in September 2000, with partial implementation of the second stage reduction in July 2001 with regulators proceeding to reduce regulators' cost. Taking into account market requirements, full liberalisation of brokerage commission will be fully implemented in July 2002.

The KLSE has also embarked on steps to improve the efficiency and effectiveness of the clearing and settlement process, with the introduction of the Clearing Guarantee Fund by end 2001 to further minimise systemic risks.

The efficient operations of a modern exchange are dependent on the utilisation of current technology and the adoption of market practices. Towards this end, the KLSE has set out to ensure that technology drives the facilities and infrastructure provided to market participants. KLSE-LINK, an online information dissemination system of announcements by public listed companies, benefits both the public listed companies in the submission of announcements online, and investors with a convenient and timely access to these announcements via the Internet.

The KLSE also realises that facilities offered must be comprehensive to meet the need at every participant's level. Recognising the role of institutional investors, the KLSE introduced the Institutional Settlement Service (ISS) for the benefit of this group of participants. ISS provides this group direct access to the clearing and settlement facilities and allows same day settlement for both cash and securities traded on the KLSE, thus minimising perceived settlement risks.

In December 2000, the KLSE implemented a shorter settlement period to further reduce systemic risk within the industry, by replacing the previous T+5 settlement period with the T+3 settlement period.

MAXIMISING USE OF RESOURCES

To ensure that the domestic market is well prepared to face the challenges posed by globalisation and liberalisation, the KLSE on its part contributed towards strengthening the local market by consolidating and maximising the use of resources to enhance competitiveness.

The KLSE had earlier acquired the Kuala Lumpur Options and Financial Futures Exchange (KLOFFE), which went on to merge with the Commodities Exchange of Malaysia (COMMEX) to create a single derivatives exchange called the Malaysia Derivatives Exchange Bhd (MDEX).

In addition, the KLSE has also seen the potential of developing an international exchange to provide services for the international market through the launch of the Labuan International Financial Exchange (LFX) in November 2000. In moving ahead, the KLSE has commenced efforts for the Malaysian Exchange of Securities Dealing and Automated Quotation (MESDAQ) to join the KLSE Group.

To rationalise and consolidate market intermediaries, existing stockbroking companies were offered the opportunity to become Universal Brokers. Some stockbroking companies have completed or are in the process of merging with each other. The major advantages of becoming a Universal Broker would be the ability to provide a wider range of services in the financial services industry and to establish branches to operate its business. This move is to ensure the stockbroking companies will continue to be competitive in the local market when it is liberalised, together with making local institutions stronger and more capable of competing at the international level.

THE CAPITAL MARKET MASTERPLAN

In February 2001, the Securities Commission released the Capital Market Master Plan (CMP) which has substantial input from KLSE in providing a blueprint to guide the strategic positioning and future direction of the Malaysian capital market over the next ten years. The CMP's main objective is to create a capital market structure that facilitates and promotes a more efficient mobilisation and allocation of funds.

The KLSE Group has been taking a proactive role in implementing the recommendations contained in the CMP.

In fact, work on some of the recommendations has commenced as early as in 1998, reflected by the KLSE's lead role in pursuing the consolidation of market institutions, as mentioned earlier, reducing transaction costs, and enhancing market regulations and infrastructure.

Towards ensuring that the objectives of the CMP are met, the KLSE has established a team to manage, supervise and coordinate the implementation of the CMP recommendations.

THE FUTURE OF THE KLSE

In constantly reviewing and updating itself, the KLSE is set to face the challenges of the global market place and an increasingly liberalised securities market environment.

Whilst measures and initiatives have been identified, the KLSE will continue to capitalise on its strength in pairing the best of human resources with the best of technology advancement in ensuring an Exchange which will be consistently efficient, cost-effective and modern, for all times.

Information and Communications Technology (ICT)

Communications

In High Gear into the Knowledge Society

Datuk Amar Leo Moggie
Minister
Ministry of Energy, Communications and Multimedia

The world has witnessed fundamental economic transformations over the past centuries, each one bringing significant implications and changes to the nature and structure of society.

From agriculture and rural communities to industrialisation and bustling cities, to science, innovations and new technology that spawn cybercities and the wired economy, to a knowledge society that thrives and prospers on information, skills and knowledge. These are facets of the foundation that is already paving our transition to 21st Century Malaysia.

Indeed, these are exciting times for the economics of information and knowledge, as we hail the advent of the Knowledge Society. The extraordinarily powerful role of Information and Communications Technology (ICT) has made this possible. Today, it is globally recognised that good infrastructure and a comprehensive development of ICT are the prerequisites and enablers that determine the success of a country's transformation into a knowledge society.

The potential of ICT is limitless, its opportunities tremendous. Let us take the Internet for example. No technology has ever attracted users faster than the Internet, webbing for itself a base of 10 million users worldwide within the space of just five years. Its explosive growth rate was further spurred by the World Wide Web which gave the Internet its friendly face, and by the availability of the web browser, that allowed many types of information residing in computers throughout the world to be linked and easily accessed.

But technology is merely a tool of the new economy. Its intrinsic and salient value is only realised by our readiness and ability to utilise it creatively and innovatively for the attainment, generation, production and distribution of the necessary data and information into knowledge that can contribute to the creation of new values in the quality of our lives and in the economy.

DATA, INFORMATION AND KNOWLEDGE

We may ask ourselves, what is knowledge and how do we differentiate knowledge from data or information? According to Jagabandhu Acharya (CEO of Total Knowledge Management Pvt. Ltd. in Bangalore, India), data are statements about reality or about other data, while information is meaningful, organised and systematised data. Knowledge, on the other hand, involves human interaction with information.

Thus, what resides in books and magazines does not in itself constitute knowledge, anymore than the information on the Internet or the World Wide Web. They are merely codification and representations of information. Information, however, becomes knowledge when human beings interact with it. This means that knowledge is just a piece of information until we appropriate it, interpret it, contextualise it by placing it in relation to other knowledge we already own and finally internalise it by making it a part of our own belief system. Knowledge creation, according to Acharya, is innovation.

Therefore, a farmer in the e-Bario community project, for example, may individually retrieve information on better farming methods from the Internet, internalise it and link it to his previous knowledge or other information about modern farming that he had acquired. He then processes it and produces knowledge which he may reject, accept, re-construct or hold as his own. As knowledge is essentially social and universal in nature, it may be shared with his colleague in the Sipitang Internet Village project, who processes the same information and who may either agree with, reject or modify it, each subsequently developing their own respective knowledge.

KNOWLEDGE AND THE KNOWLEDGE SOCIETY

In the creation of a knowledge society, the development of four types of knowledge are critical, namely, "know-what", "know-why", "know-how" and "know-who" (OECD, 1996). The "know-what" refers to knowledge about facts; "know-why" refers to scientific knowledge which is the key to innovation and technical progress; "know-how" refers to skills or the capability to do something, and "know-who" refers to information about who knows what; and who knows how to do what. Through the development of the four types of knowledge, human or intellectual capital is augmented. The use of human capital in production processes and the process of generating and re-generating knowledge are in fact the key sources of wealth in a knowledge society.

The significance of ICT in this context and in driving the emergence of a knowledge society lies in its ability to codify information and knowledge and in its pervasiveness, its capacity and its capabilities to contribute to the diffusion of knowledge. Certainly, with good ICT infrastructure in place, it is possible for a country to nurture the human capital needed for the development of a knowledge-based society. It is therefore pertinent that we have both good ICT infrastructure, as well as a society that cherishes and practises the culture of lifelong learning and continuous improvement. By this we mean a society that is creative, innovative and diligent, and individuals with the capacity to acquire, maintain and develop the necessary skills and competencies to adapt to new technologies and take advantage of the knowledge and opportunities arising from them. Essentially, those who know how to produce information and knowledge better than others, reap the rewards.

These needs will undoubtedly create transitions and adjustment challenges on individuals, the society and country. As ICT affects not just our work or organisational structure but the very nature of everyday life itself, naturally there will be concerns.

These include issues such as the digital divide, the requirement for skills and human resource development, fulfilling the demand for knowledge workers and the encouragement of individual participation through the promotion of lifelong learning, knowledge seeking and the development of creativity and innovation.

The Digital Divide

To address the digital divide and ensure the ICT culture permeates all strata of the society, every one of us should have equal opportunity to embrace the knowledge society. Besides access to basic education, there is the need to ensure balanced and equitable access to info-communications for every citizen, including the less privileged and the marginalised. Disparity in access would only deepen the digital gap between rural and urban areas and communities, between the haves and have-nots, and between those that are production-based and knowledge-based.

The main challenge here is in ensuring an efficient and comprehensive communications infrastructure that can support and facilitate the transformation into a knowledge-based society. This basically goes down to the issue of ensuring connectivity for the common people. For the country to shift to an economy and a society driven by knowledge, people must be connected. The nation's network environment must also be highly reliable and stable, so that the issue of generating the confidence necessary in a network environment can be easily overcome. Only then can the task of developing IT literacy and retraining, coupled with the democratisation of education, be made easier.

Our move is thus towards the establishment of clear and effective programmes that not only encourage individual participation and learning, but also contribute to balanced development. To enable people from all walks of life to embrace the information-driven culture, the cost of using the infrastructure, as well as the cost of possessing the necessary hardware such as the PC, needs to be at a level affordable by the people. This is another mounting challenge that concerns us today. Since the requirements of each category of users are different, the needs of these users and the quality of services provided by the network providers are being monitored. For example, besides the normal dial-up services using the phone lines, there is the need to ensure broadband and other multimedia infrastructure communications facilities are available, as these facilities are necessary to support cutting-edge solutions and applications which require high-speed transmission of information.

Experiences of other countries revealed that ICT, when efficiently and effectively applied, could also increase the value-added along the value chain of the outputs of an economy, both in the form of new or better products or services. In fact, an economy is considered to have successfully moved from one that is production-based to one that is knowledge-based when one, if not all, of its sectors has achieved substantial infusion of knowledge content and recorded higher productivity improvements. The advancement of technology has also made it possible for greater development and creation of knowledge in human endeavours, whether for economic, social or leisure pursuits.

PRIVATE AND PUBLIC SECTOR PARTNERSHIP

The fact that knowledge is globally valuable, the challenge will be to find the best "partnership" between the private and public sectors that will successfully facilitate and promote the establishment of a knowledge society. In Malaysia, the development of the ICT infrastructure is primarily driven by the private sector. Our public sector policy thrust is to ensure efficient and sufficient services through the promotion of a competitive market environment. However, as the market is relatively small, we take cognisance of the risk of destructive competition if there are too many players. Through the Communications and Multimedia Act 1998, the market structure has thus been redesigned into four segments, namely Network Facilities, Network Service, Application Service and Content Application Service.

In doing so, the Government is able to have clear policy positions along the value-chain, from upstream activities such as infrastructure facilities development which are capital intensive, to those downstream activities such as Internet Access Services and Voice-Over-Internet Protocol which ride on the network infrastructure. A more stringent regulatory control has also been adopted to avoid unproductive competition, both in terms of market entry by limiting the number of network providers, as well as stringent licensing regulations and conditions. However, as the activities move along the value-chain towards the downstream activities, the thrust of the current policy is to enable and encourage competition.

This "partnership" is further generated in our efforts to address the problem of digital divide. One notable initiative in ensuring that info-communications is not confined to certain quarters and localities only, is the policy to have a more effective Universal Service Provision (USP). Plans are afoot to set up an USP Fund which will be managed by an independent regulator, i.e. the Communications and Multimedia Commission (CMC). The USP Fund will be an effective means to ensure that special efforts are made to develop the ICT infrastructure to cover areas that are uneconomic or to cater to the needs of the disadvantaged groups of the society. The USP programme will also address the needs of rural schools for ICT infrastructure.

As the new regulatory and licensing structure makes it possible to address the issues and challenges based on different stages of the value-chain, efforts will be taken to address the needs of each segment more effectively. For example, to explore the possibility of adopting new and emerging technologies for infrastructure roll-out to the rural areas, the Government has allowed the testing of new solutions based on wireless and satellite technologies. In some remote areas, especially those in Sabah and Sarawak, where traditional solutions based on deployment of fixed line roll-out are not physically and economically possible, the use of new technologies, if found suitable, would be adopted for mass roll-out under the USP programme.

POLICY AND LEGISLATION

The Government has put in place the necessary policy and legislation in enabling effective implementation of infrastructure development that will facilitate the country's transformation to a knowledge society. Apart from the Communications and Multimedia Act 1998, which addresses the regulatory and licensing requirements and issues of convergence, several other cyber laws to facilitate transformation have also been put in place. These are the Digital Signature Act 1997, Computer Crimes Act 1997, as well as a proposed bill on Personal Data Protection. The legislation on

Personal Data Protection is aimed at creating consumer confidence necessary for the adoption of network-based services. Such legislation is needed to facilitate e-commerce and other online transactions that have yet to achieve widespread acceptance by the people in this country.

Corollary to the needs for the protection of personal data is the need to harmonise related laws and regulations that are being enforced by other ministries and agencies. As there are about 800 federal laws that need to be studied and to ensure that the study is speedily and comprehensively carried out, the Ministry has appointed a consultant to study and identify relevant laws that need to be amended. The findings of this study will then serve as baseline information for the respective agencies to further work on the amendments required so that they can use ICT and exploit the World Wide Web as a means to deliver services to the public.

FUTURE DEVELOPMENT

With the third generation mobile or IMT-2000 and the promises of the many facilities and advantages that it can provide, many advanced countries in Europe did, in the beginning, anticipate the new technology would lead to enormous uptake. The third generation (3G) mobile service is said to further propel the adoption of the Internet as a platform for business transactions or Mobile Commerce. As the Malaysian mobile service market has yet to reach maturity, the Government is adopting a more cautious stance in handling the issue of 3G implementation so that our national resources, both in terms of spectrum and the network infrastructure, will be efficiently utilised. In fact, currently, there is a lack of content that could effectively drive the usage of mobile services, even in the current environment. In fact, the Wireless Application Protocol or WAP and GPRS (General Packet Radio Services) are still very much at their infant stage. Even countries in Europe are lately, a little less euphoric of the 3G, as reality has reduced the hype attached to it.

CONCLUSION

The Government is conscious of the need to focus on the development of infrastructure to support and facilitate the creation of a knowledge society. However, it must be emphasised that provision of comprehensive and efficient infrastructure alone will not increase the knowledge applications in the output production of a nation. New technology such as ICT is only an enabler. It is the human factor that will determine the success of our transformation initiatives in the development of a Knowledge Society and a 21st Century Malaysia.

Kulim Hi-Tech Park
The Science City of the Future

Kulim Technology Park Corporation

As the national pilot project in high technology development, the Kulim Hi-Tech Park is a custom-designed industrial Park geared for high technology and R&D companies intending to set up a base in the Asia-Pacific region. Boasting an unmatched combination of strategic location, superb support facilities and quality human resources, the Park is perfect for leading-edge hi-tech as well as research and development activities.

Attests Yoshihiko Nakazato, President, Fuji Electric, "We have set up our operations in Kulim Hi-Tech Park for three years now, and we are very satisfied and happy with the excellent infrastructure provided here. We strongly believe that we have made a good decision in locating our business in the Park." Says CY Hannon, President & CEO, Silterra, "We are here because Kulim Hi-Tech Park has all the ingredients to become the world's leading technology park, especially in meeting the stringent requirements of wafer fab activities and we only want the best. The Park's superb infrastructure, complemented by a wide range of support services and industries, is exceptionally suitable for companies like ours."

According to Gulsher Greewal, Managing Director, Intel Products Sdn Bhd, "When we expanded our business in Kulim Hi-

Tech Park in the last couple of years, we were able to attract sufficient trainable technical workforce to meet our production needs. And the business environment here has been very conducive for high technology manufacturing."

Apart from the encouraging testimonies from these satisfied investors, the Park also performs well in comparison to its regional peers. Strategic Information Services ranks the Park second in a list of top Asian High Technology Parks, behind the Wuxi-Singapore Industrial Park in Shanghai, China. Corporate Compass lists the Park at number four in a list of Asia's top business, industrial and technology parks, behind Singapore's International Business and Science Parks and Taiwan's Hsinchu Science Industrial Park.

Developed by Kulim Technology Park Corporation (KTPC), the Kulim Hi-Tech Park is an outstanding industrial landmark in the state of Kedah Darul Aman. The Park's unique design features six dedicated zones—Industrial, Urban, Residential/Commercial, Amenity/Recreational, Research and Development and Training, and Institutional.

KTPC, a wholly-owned subsidiary of the Kedah State Development Corporation, has successfully managed the Park. The United States is the Park's biggest investor, followed by Japan, Taiwan, local Malaysian companies and Singapore. There are also 19 support companies of which nine are from the Silicon Valley, USA.

TARGET INDUSTRIES

From the outset, the Park has specifically targeted only hi-tech companies or organisations heavily involved in R&D.

In the Malaysian context, high-technology companies are defined as those engaged in promoting activities or products in the areas of new and emerging technologies.

In general, the Park's target industries are advanced microelectronics, medical and scientific instrumentation, biotechnology, process control and automation, advanced manufacturing technologies, electro-optics and non-linear optics, telecommunications, optoelectronics, software engineering, alternative energy sources, aerospace and new and emerging technologies. Strategic industries of national importance are also of interest to the Park. These would be projects with heavy capital investment of not less than RM100 million and high technology capable of generating extensive spin-off benefits with significant impact on the Malaysian economy.

Manufacturing pioneers in the Park include semiconductor bluechip Intel Products (M) Sdn Bhd, Advanced Disk Technology Sdn Bhd and Silterra (M) Sdn Bhd.

Elsewhere, MIMOS is developing an electronics centre while Sirim Bhd operates an Advanced Material Research Centre that serves as a catalyst for technological development in the Park. Electrical and electronics projects dominate the Park while metal fabrication and chemical projects are also represented.

In order to qualify for the Park, interested investors must fulfil certain stringent criteria. First, local R&D expenditure should be at least 1% of gross sales on an annual basis. However, companies are allowed a grace period of 3 years from the date of operations or commencement of business to comply with this requirement. Second, science and technical graduates must make up at least 7% of the total workforce. These graduates must be at least first-degree holders.

INCENTIVES AND PARK ATTRACTIONS

The myriad of attractions at the Park, in tandem with a package of generous incentives from both the Kedah State Government and the Federal Government, has drawn investors to the Park.

Unbeatable Location

Encompassing almost 1,450 hectares, with more than 400 hectares already acquired for expansion, the Park is smack in the centre of the Northern region and boasts an enviable access to important transport nodes. It is situated near the North-South and East-West Highways, and is directly linked to the latter via a four-lane primary access road. In addition, the Park is only 26 kilometres from the North Butterworth Container Terminal of Penang Port and 36 kilometres from Penang's Bayan Lepas International Airport. The Park also falls within the Indonesia-Malaysia-Thailand Growth Triangle.

State-of-the-Art Infrastructure

To date, KTPC has invested RM1.5 billion in providing a state-of-the-art infrastructure necessary for the smooth running of an industrial park. Northern Utilities Resources, an independent power provider, ensures that the Park enjoys a reliable, stable and quality power supply. Ample pure water is supplied from three specially designed concrete reservoirs with a maximum capacity of 85,000 cubic metres per day. High-speed telecommunication facilities backed by fibre optic cables are available with an initial capacity of 60,000 lines. The Park provides ready facilities for the storage of scheduled industrial wastes that meet environmental protection standards. Industrial gases are available via an underground gas pipeline system run by a joint venture company involving Sitt Tatt Industrial Gases Sdn Bhd, Air Products Inc and Malaysian Oxygen Bhd.

Social and Institutional Facilities

Quality of life is an essential element of the Park, and the designers have included a sprawling satellite township in the

Residential/Commercial Zone worth RM600 million and spanning 298 hectares.

This township consists of different categories of housing, 284 shophouses, 165 office lots, a commercial building and a shopping centre. The different categories of housing consist of 3,104 units of low and medium-cost terrace houses, 1,044 units of semi-detached houses, 3,040 apartments, 950 flats and 1,044 bungalows. Other amenities include a shopping centre and medical and recreational facilities. For recreation, there is also an international standard championship golf course, a majestic clubhouse comprising first-class resort facilities, while cinemas, cultural centres and a theme park are in the planning stage. At the same time, more than 25% of the Park's land area has been reserved for a green lung in the form of a nature park. The fire station, police station, post office, local authority and hospital are located in the Institutional Zone, which covers 36.48 hectares.

Research and Development and Training

Several hectares have been set aside for the R&D and Training Zone, which aims to provide support research facilities to hi-tech industrialists in the Park, thereby encouraging them to interact with other industrialists, R&D institutions and local entrepreneurs.

The R&D block occupies 8.7 hectares of land, and 2.02 hectares have been taken up by MIMOS to develop an electronics centre and to be used as a northern branch office. SIRIM operates an Advanced Material Research Centre on four hectares of land.

A TechnoCentre has also been set up in this zone, boasting a total built-up area of 200,000 square feet. The TechnoCentre will house incubator companies, machines and laboratories. Proposed facilities include a CAD/CAM lab, a robotics and automation lab, electronics testing facilities, a metrology lab, a virtual manufacturing lab, a material analysis lab, and a tissue culture and molecular biology lab.

In the same zone, training in professional and technical fields is conveniently met by Kulim Advanced Education Centre, which offers courses in electrical and mechanical engineering and computer integration.

A Polytechnic offers training at certificate and diploma levels while a Malaysian-Spanish collaboration, the Malaysian-Spanish Institute, is being constructed. Some 6.88 hectares of land have been allotted for an International School designed to cater to children from Year 1 to Year 12. A Sri Bestari Kindergarten and Childcare Centre now operates on a 1.35-hectare piece of land, while the first smart school of its kind catering to primary and secondary education is under construction.

Further afield, companies based in the Park can also tap the academic brainpower available at Universiti Sains Malaysia and Universiti Utara Malaysia, two leading institutions of higher education located within easy driving distance.

INCENTIVES

In order to attract investors to the park, the Kedah government offers attractive incentives at state-level, such as cheap land costs and reduced assessment and water rates. For hi-tech manufacturing, land is priced at RM15 psf while similar acreage costs only RM12 psf for R&D and training and educational purposes.

Industrial land carries a leasehold period of 60 years plus an option to renew for another 39 years. Investors enjoy a lower assessment rate of 8% for the first three years and a reduced water rate of RM1 per cubic metre, also for the first three years.

Similarly, the Federal Government offers great incentives for hi-tech projects, such as total exemption from corporate tax at the statutory income level for 5 years, and a 60% investment tax allowance on qualifying capital expenditure for 5 years. Investors also enjoy flexible employment procedures pertaining to foreign scientists or skilled personnel and approval to open foreign exchange accounts. R&D projects also enjoy a basket of incentives. Manufacturing companies conducting in-house R&D get double deduction on revenue expenditure incurred on research approved by the Ministry of Finance, and a research allowance of 50% on qualifying expenditure related to R&D activities for 10 years.

Approved independent R&D companies or institutions enjoy 5 years tax exemption for carrying out research activities in a specified industry. Dividends are also tax-exempt while losses incurred can be accumulated and carried forward for tax relief purposes. Both types of R&D projects also enjoy an Industrial Building Allowance for buildings used for industrial purposes, and exemption on import duty and sales tax on machinery and equipment used for R&D.

CONCLUSION

To date, total investments by companies based in the Kulim Hi-Tech Park have surpassed RM16 billion. Given its excellent location, support facilities, quality human resources and the support of both the Malaysian Federal and State Governments, the Park will continue to attract hi-tech companies with a strong emphasis on R&D from around the world.

Malaysia
A More Confident Voice in the 21st Century

Tan Sri Dr Lim Kok Wing
Founder & President
LimKokWing Institute of Creative Technology

News and information are the 21st century's most valuable commodities. There is a voracious demand for it, and with the Internet explosion and cross-merger of media companies to form giant monopolies, we certainly have an overwhelming supply.

But we must not allow ourselves to be overwhelmed by it. And therein lies our challenge.

In Malaysia, just as in any other part of the developing world, media companies are trying to find their footing in a quicksand global environment. The boom time for Malaysian media—which began in the early 1980s with the first private television channel (TV3)—gave Malaysians a variety of news and entertainment to choose from. From the two government-run TV stations and one private channel, today there are two more terrestrial stations and more than 30 satellite TV channels. There are countless radio stations, and still countless more magazines.

And then the Internet arrived on our shores. This was followed closely by media juggernauts wielding tremendous control on news, information and entertainment content worldwide.

By any measure, the global media organisations of the 21st century are the stuff of early 20th century science fiction. It is a world where online services, media and entertainment are rapidly converging. While it provides unprecedented access to all kinds of content for the public, that content is dominated by a small number of super-powerful, mostly US-based, transnational corporations, advertisers and billionaire owners.

Malaysian airwaves are alive and buzzing with a great deal of content on almost anything and everything. News, views and entertainment are pouring out of everything but our faucets. The Government—in its push to bring the people into the Information Age—has committed to no censorship on the Internet to build a knowledge-savvy society. Its IT agenda is one of the most comprehensive and sophisticated in Southeast Asia. The reason for this is simple: the Government wants the people to participate fully, and compete effectively, in the digital economy. No more playing second fiddle to anyone.

Still, a small nation like Malaysia has to find a way to be heard above the noise. That is, by all current accounts, something of a Herculean task, when one considers the following facts and figures.

GLOBAL MEDIA GIANTS DOMINATE

2001 began with the creation of the world's largest media company when America Online (AOL) merged with media giant Time Warner, making this the largest merger in corporate history. The deal combined AOL's online services with Time Warner's vast media and cable assets.

Time Warner—already the world's largest media company prior to this deal—operates five businesses covering cable networks, publishing, music, films and cable systems. With its stable of world-class brands, including the CNN News Group and the Home Box Office (HBO) movie channel, it controls many of the most valuable franchises in television news and entertainment. CNN International is the premier global television news channel beaming via 10 satellites, to over 200 nations and more than 100 million subscribers.

In publishing, its *Time* magazine is hugely popular, as well as its best-selling books, and informative web sites. In music, the Warner Music Group is one of the world's leading music entertainment companies.

In movies, its Warner Bros and New Line Cinema produce movies, television programmes and animation. And finally, Time Warner Cable is said to be the most technologically advanced cable operator.

In 1990, the then two largest media firms in the world—Time Warner Inc and Disney—generated around 15% of their income outside the United States. By 1997, that figure had risen to about 35%. Within the next decade, both firms expect to do the majority of their business abroad.

Disney is the closest challenger. Today, 31% of its income is derived from broadcasting, 23% from theme parks and the balance from creative content—which means films, publishing and merchandising. The company has announced that it plans to expand aggressively overseas through joint ventures with local firms or other global players, or through further acquisitions. Disney's stated goal is to expand its non-US share of revenues from 23% in 1995 to 50% into the new millennium.

Its global television activities are managed by Disney/ABC International Television. It also operates ABC's ESPN—which has three US cable channels, a radio network with more than 400 affiliates, and ESPN Sports-Zone website, one of the most popular websites on the Internet. ESPN International dominates televised sport, broadcasting on a 24-hour basis in 21 languages to over 165 countries.

be more important to the world in the next 50 years than in the last 50. The huge populations—which will collectively make Asia the world's largest consumer region—is attracting the world to this region.

Asia cannot and will not be ignored because of its consumer clout. Do we then have the never-before opportunity to turn things around? Can we use this clout to have more say about how we are portrayed? About how our cultures and issues are analysed? About having our voices heard more clearly?

TELLING OUR STORY CLEARLY

I firmly believe this will be our golden opportunity to make a difference in Western media's biased reporting of Asia.

In news and entertainment, we need not look to the Western content as the model. We have a chance to project our stories to the world and that we must do well.

Our voice will be heard around the world to change perceptions and notions about a part of the world which is still very much misunderstood by the mass Western audience. Our voices—for so long drowned out by the might of the big media companies—will finally be heard because they need us.

Without a doubt, the new era requires a new kind of media. And the local media are undergoing a metamorphosis of their own in order to stay relevant within the context of global media content. Theirs will always be a role that is relevant—as no international media is interested in the issues and concerns of one nation's populace.

I believe our model of journalism will continue to be to work with the government to build national consensus, though it is today a more analytical and questioning Press.

The national Press, since Independence, has been an instrument of nation-building. These values are proudly kept by Malaysians, though they are certainly different from Western media values which take on a more confrontational approach with the government. It is also natural that Malaysia's media interests differ from Western ones. Like most of Asia, Malaysia's media interests are more tuned into communal activities.

BEING RELEVANT TO THE NET GENERATION

Change in the Malaysian media has been occurring—driven mainly by the Internet explosion. Mainstream media realise that in order to survive, they have to be relevant to the Net Generation. A generation that is well-educated, worldly, and who increasingly seek their news and information from the World Wide Web, where magazines, chat rooms and forums provide alternative interpretation of national events.

The sprouting of alternative sources of information on the Internet attracts the Net-savvy generation, the generation that will drive the country's agenda into the 21st century. The Net generation actively seeks out information, rather than passively receiving it. The Net Generation, not the owners or editors of papers, are increasingly selecting their own content, and that wave of change will continue to impact on the Malaysian media well into the 21st century. After all, if you are used to a greater range of options from which to choose your news, the importance of who owns what becomes less relevant.

Because of this and the greater diversity of opinions, we see now a greater willingness among media owners to make some important changes in keeping with the news of a changing society.

A MORE CONFIDENT AND ANALYTICAL MEDIA

The media is more confident and more analytical. They discuss once taboo subjects—like sex education, AIDS and domestic violence—more openly. They are more willing to push the envelope to get discussions going on issues such as political differences, and question the behaviour (or rather misbehaviour) of public personalities. While this does not mean it necessarily takes the Western adversarial approach, it is unfair to call it a sycophantic press. We are critical and sceptical, but not cynical.

Yet, the language of the mainstream media is also reflective of Asian values. We treat our leaders with respect, even when we disagree with them.

On the other side of the coin, one wonders how much goodwill there is towards Asia in the international media? Prime Minister Dato Seri Dr Mahathir Mohamad has led a crusade to better balance the relationship between the developing and developed world, taking on the mantle of Asia's spokesman to defend the rights of poorer nations.

He has been vilified in the international media for speaking out against illegal currency trading during the Asian currency crisis. In many international forums, he is often the bold, yet lone Voice of Asia, saying what many prefer to be left unsaid and in the process earning many nasty nicknames and attacks from Western powers as well as the Western media.

The West has often used its own media values as a benchmark against the media values of other nations.

Perhaps, with the global media, it will have no choice but to back down and realise that it needs to be more open to the way others prefer to conduct their business.

PROVIDING EDUCATION AND DIRECTION

Historically, the media has played a pivotal role in Malaysia's growth. Newspapers in the early days were the catalyst that sparked the flames of anti-colonialism, leading to our Independence as well as those in many parts of this continent.

We have come far. Today, the nation is among the world's most dynamic IT nations. It is a country equipping itself with the latest IT technologies, in order to have a significant impact on business, media and communications in a 21st century environment.

The Government has placed great emphasis on its people becoming a key player in the Digital Age. The credit must go to Dr Mahathir for having initiated and then driving the country's IT transformation.

No Malaysian can deny that he has almost singlehandedly pushed for the nation to be at the forefront of the Information Age, when many other developing nations are still languishing behind. This, against the backdrop of a UNESCO report which said that 80% of the world's population still does not have access to basic telephone infrastructure, makes our achievement even more amazing.

Dr Mahathir has also committed to the world that there would be no censorship of the Internet in Malaysia, a decision which took great courage, when one considers that the Internet—for all its better qualities—is also home to a lot of rudeness, vulgarity and nonsense. With no censorship on the Internet, Malaysians have access to all the Internet offers—including its very real dark side.

But the Internet is the most widely accessible and tangible part of the new technology, and that has given it respectability. We are now a nation seeking to master and use these technologies to strengthen our nation, and to have our voice heard around the world. This demands a better-educated journalist, one with a much better grasp of cultures and languages and political systems, one able to see not one or two, but often many sides of every question. In Asia, journalists are not just entertainers, they are more educators and they have a certain social responsibility.

The Internet will be the defining voice of Asia. It is the world's window to Asia, setting in motion a wave change of attitude and perceptions as people from around the world mix with Asians through its many channels.

The world has a lot to learn about us if they are to understand what makes us tick. It's about time.

Smart Partnership
Riding the Wave of High Technology

Dr Ahmed Tasir Lope Pihie
Chief Executive
Malaysian Industry-Government Group for High Technology

Malaysia is now entering a new phase of economic growth, one that places a premium on competitiveness, productivity and sustainability. Its successful foray into the realm of becoming a knowledge-based economy and its continuing efforts to further penetrate the global markets will be spearheaded by a total commitment to a high technology-driven growth strategy, underpinned by world-class human resources, physical infrastructure and financial systems.

Acknowledging the importance of technology as the catalyst for economic growth and prosperity, Malaysia aims to establish a scientific and progressive society, innovative and forward-looking, as outlined in Vision 2020. As the nation builds a more innovation-based economy, a greater degree of collaboration is needed to give industry insights and strength to compete. Therefore, the Malaysian Industry-Government Group for High Technology, i.e. MIGHT, was established under the Office of the Science Adviser, Prime Minister's Department, in 1993 to serve the nation in shaping competency in high technology for sustainable development.

Being an independent and non-profit organisation, MIGHT operationalises the concept of Malaysia Incorporated and serves as a neutral platform for consensus building between the Government and Industry on issues relating to technology and business. Thus, MIGHT is aptly made up of members comprising key organisations from both the public and private sectors, namely ministries, government agencies, research institutes, universities as well as large corporations, both local and multinational, and small and medium-sized industries representing the broad spectrum of high-growth sectors.

Under the patronage of the Honourable Prime Minister, MIGHT is steered by a high-powered group under the joint chairmanship of a prominent corporate leader and the Science Adviser in the Prime Minister's Department. The Board of Directors comprises captains of industry and senior Government officials.

The partnership, MIGHT, mobilises and manages collective technological efforts which are beyond the resources of an individual organisation, addresses the gap that exists between R&D and the marketplace, as well as promotes the interests of the industry to integrate technology into their operations and strategic plans. Overall, it helps to develop an ecosystem that can best identify technology and business opportunities for the country.

MIGHT accomplishes its objectives through prospecting, which is a mechanism to search for business and investment opportunities through harnessing strategic research and technology. Through prospecting, we have made significant contributions in charting the high technology development agenda of the country. Significant inroads and progress have been made in the automotive, aerospace, advanced materials, construction and housing, herbal, pharmaceutical, road haulage and telecommunication industries. Forging ahead, MIGHT will now move beyond identifying opportunities and overall technology management to actively engage in nurturing home-grown technologies and companies coupled to technology acquisition.

Our experience in prospecting has provided us with invaluable understanding and insight into the development of high-technology industries. It has encouraged us to embark on related development programmes by clearly defining our present technological competencies and capabilities and to suggest future strategic areas.

The preparation of this route has been termed "The National Technology Mapping Programme." Through this programme we have been able to identify strategic areas of Science and Technology, while at the same time charting the most effective path for maximisation of economic and social benefits for the country.

The complementary role of the Government and the private sector for nation-building implied the need for new forms of interaction and for more intensive cooperation and consultation among the private sector. This enhanced cooperativeness has been termed "Smart Partnership", and this has emerged as an important component of technology management. Smart Partnership has now become the new metaphor for business relationships, which can operate at both national and international levels. It is about creating limitless opportunities and wealth that is shared, sustainable and that allows all the participants to function in the global economy. MIGHT, together with its London-based sister organisation, Commonwealth Partnership for Technology Management, has been actively promoting Smart Partnership through the organisation of international and national Smart Partnership dialogues, i.e. the Langkawi International Dialogue (LID) and the National Smart Partnership Dialogue (NSPD) respectively.

Since the inauguration of LID in 1995, a series of LIDs has been organised to address many issues of concern, including "Managing Economic Recovery for Shared Prosperity" and "Global Trends and Emerging Economies." NSPDs, on the other hand, have been addressing various issues of national interest such as "Economic Recovery through Smart Partnership", "Youth in National Development: Preparing, for Future Challenges," as well as "Development of Human Resources for the K-economy."

Prospecting through networking and Smart Partnership has helped us all to move forward. As a partnership company, MIGHT will maintain its objectives and professionalism when synthesising wishes, visions and expectations into collective action for the development of the high technology industry in Malaysia. We are always open to listen to your suggestions.

MEASAT

An Integral Part of Malaysia's 21st Century Communications Infrastructure

Binariang Satellite Systems Sdn Bhd

Binariang Satellite Systems Sdn Bhd (BSS) is the owner and operator of Malaysia's first satellite system, Malaysia East Asia Satellite (MEASAT), which has a regional footprint. BSS' commitment in ensuring that Malaysia becomes a regional telecommunications hub under Vision 2020 is as strong today as when BSS' first commenced its operations five years ago in 1996.

The MEASAT system comprises two high-powered HS376 spacecraft built by Boeing Satellite Systems, Inc. (formerly known as Hughes Space and Communications Company). Both spacecraft provide high-powered C-band and Ku-band digital capacity to meet the increasing Internet, broadcasting and telecommunications needs of Malaysia and the other countries within the Asian region.

MEASAT represents a technology breakthrough with its advanced high-powered Ku-band transponders specifically designed for Direct-To-User (DTU) services. MEASAT-1 is the first satellite in the region to provide digital transmission using 60cm receive dish. This technology breakthrough marked the beginning of a new era in the provision of DTU broadcasting services in the region.

MEASAT-1 was successfully launched to the orbital slot of 91.5 degrees East longitude on January 13, 1996, from Kourou, French Guiana. It has 12 C-band and 5 Ku-band transponders. The high-powered C-band transponders of MEASAT-1 provide technical and commercial benefits to all regional network operators who require broadband capacity for Internet, video, data and voice services.

MEASAT-2, which was successfully placed at the orbital slot of 148 degrees East longitude on November 14, 1996, has 9 Ku-band transponders that cover Malaysia, Indonesia, Eastern Australia, Vietnam, Taiwan and the Philippines. MEASAT-2 also has 4 C-band transponders covering the Asian region as well as Australia and Hawaii.

The MEASAT Satellite Control Centre (MSCC), the nerve centre of the MEASAT system, is located in Pulau Langkawi. The MSCC is manned entirely by Malaysian technical specialists comprising spacecraft controllers, ground engineers and orbit analysts.

The fast-growing communications, entertainment and information industries in the region have created increased demand for satellite capacity. BSS intends to add to its existing fleet of two satellites in the near future in order to meet such demand. The future satellites will not only provide additional space segment capacity but also expand the existing regional coverage. The proposed MEASAT-3, which will be co-located with MEASAT-1 at the orbital slot of 91.5 degrees longitude, will also serve to back up the existing satellite.

BSS, through the Malaysian Government, has secured orbital slots through frequency fillings worldwide. These orbital slots provide the basis for the development of a global MEASAT system and position Malaysia as a major global hub for telecommunications and multimedia services.

The MEASAT system is set to play a significant role as one of the key components of the 21st century communications infrastructure in Malaysia.

Multimedia Super Corridor

Competing in Cyberspace

Tan Sri Dato' Dr Othman Yeop Abdullah
Executive Chairman
Multimedia Development Corporation Sdn Bhd

The accelerating growth of the Internet, coupled with rapid advancement and convergence of Information and Communications Technologies (ICT), has changed the economic and societal landscape of practically every country in the world. This has resulted in the explosion of knowledge and the advent of the Digital Economy or Knowledge Economy. Wealth creation no longer depends on natural endowments such as land or mineral resources, but on access to knowledge and information. In the knowledge economy, an increasing range of products and services are non-physical and are knowledge-based offerings, e.g. software. Most knowledge-based products obey the Law of Increasing Returns as opposed to the Law of Diminishing Returns. Value of products is enhanced through optimum usage and new applications are spun off from generic platforms. Organisations operate in a dynamic environment where change occurs rapidly and without warning. Industry borders tumble on the Internet as companies rethink their value propositions.

Two major forces are driving the transformation of the economy into knowledge-based. The first is creativity and innovation. Creativity and innovation lead to technological changes such as digitisation, convergence, broadband, Internet, etc. These changes have in turn resulted in continuously declining costs and the increasing speed of communications and computing. The second driving force is globalisation that will inevitably bring about economic liberalisation and deregulation, resulting in freer global capital and trade flows and creating vast opportunities for cross-border trade.

The combination of these two forces of change will eliminate the natural barriers of time and space. This will translate into both vast opportunities and risks in the knowledge economy and borderless world. Unbounded liberalisation in the name of deregulation and globalisation would pitch unfairly between developed and developing economies and between big and small players whose access to capital and knowledge-based technologies varies considerably. How should Malaysia respond to take advantage of the opportunities and meet the challenges?

SEIZING THE OPPORTUNITIES

Recognising the decline of its competitive advantage in the labour-intensive industries and the imminent advent of the knowledge economy, the Malaysian government launched the Multimedia Super Corridor (MSC) as a strategic initiative in August 1996 to spearhead the transformation of Malaysia into a knowledge-based economy. The MSC aims to bring about a change in Malaysia's growth path, from one driven by labour and capital-intensive industries to one led by high value-added information-based economic activities.

A two-pronged approach is undertaken to realise the vision, putting equal emphasis on both the production and the use of ICT.

The first is to create an ideal multimedia environment to attract world-class companies to use the MSC as a hub and to catalyse the growth of a highly competitive cluster of Malaysian ICT companies that will become world-class over time. The second is to promote the application of ICT by both the public and the private sectors to enhance domestic productivity and competitiveness.

PRODUCTION OF INFORMATION AND COMMUNICATIONS TECHNOLOGY

ICT is an important economic sector in its own right. First, it is a fast growing sector and its share of the economy is expected to increase over the next few decades.

For example, it is estimated that the ICT industry accounts for 8.3% of the Gross Domestic Product (GDP) of the United States. In 1998, 7.4 million or 6.1% of all American workers worked in ICT-producing industries and ICT occupations in other industries. Employment in software and computer services industries nearly doubled from 850,000 in 1992 to 1.6 million in 1998. More importantly, the ICT sector is rapidly creating high wage jobs. ICT jobs average US$58,000 a year, 85% higher than the average for the private sector. Value-added per worker in IT-producing industries grew at an annual average of 10.4% in the 1990s, far higher than in the rest of the economy (Source: Digital Economy 2000, US Department of Commerce).

The Government of Malaysia fully appreciates the growing importance of ICT both as an enabler as well as a high value-added economic activity. Over the last two decades, Malaysia has developed a large and vibrant electronics industry. The manufacturing sector currently accounts for about one-third of the GDP and exports of manufactured goods accounted for 85% of total exports. Electronics, electrical machinery and appliances accounted for some 60% of total exports, with a total annual value of RM145 billion in 1999. The

MSC will build on Malaysia's strengths in manufacturing and electronics by focusing on research and development of innovative ICT products and services, including hardware, software and multimedia content. By attracting world-class ICT companies to operate out of the MSC and by nurturing the growth of local ICT businesses, Malaysia aspires to be a meaningful player in the global ICT marketplace.

Application of Information and Communications Technology

Apart from being a growing sector of the economy, ICT has a far-reaching impact on the rest of the economy. Innovations in ICT have begun to alter the manner in which we do business and create value, often in ways that were not readily foreseeable even five years ago. In many sectors of the economy, ICT has resulted in a significant increase in productivity, enabled new business processes, and created completely new business models that alter existing value chain and industry structure. In the US, it is estimated that the ICT sector has contributed about 30% of US economic growth, and accounted for half or more of the improvement in productivity growth since 1995. Investment in ICT has also raised America's labour-productivity growth to an average of almost 3% over the past five years, double the average in the previous 20 years. Furthermore, by raising their productivity, ICT is lowering inflation in other industries. Falling ICT prices have directly pulled down average inflation by 0.5 percentage points a year.

The implementation of the seven MSC Flagship Applications provides the impetus and operational framework to promote the use of ICT in both the public and private sectors. For example, the e-Procurement project under the Electronic Government Flagship Application aims to not only greatly simplify and improve the government procurement process, but also to promote the adoption of electronic commerce and the application of ICT in supply chain management among the 30,000 suppliers of products and services to government.

As a major producer of resource-based products and manufactured goods, Malaysia is an active participant in international trade. Our international trade in 1999 amounted to some RM600 billion, equivalent to two times our GDP. Hence, Malaysian companies that are slow in adopting ICT risk being shut out of Western markets as a significant amount of international trade migrates from one-to-one transactions to online exchanges over the next few years. They will pay a heavy price if they become sidelined in the international marketplace by more Internet-savvy and information-rich competitors from other countries who control critical activities on the value chain such as Hong Kong, Korea, Taiwan, and Singapore. Such real threats are looming with the emergence of the new Internet-based business models, where the mechanics of buying and selling are moving away from one-to-one physical contact and relationships to online exchanges serving specific industries.

THE MSC

Hence, the MSC can be regarded as the next engine of growth for the Malaysian economy. It is strategic and its success or failure has far-reaching consequences for the economy. It is our response to the challenges of globalisation and the opportunities presented by digitalisation and convergence of technologies.

The MSC is multifaceted. Creation of the ideal multimedia environment involves the development of both "hard" and "soft" infrastructures. These include physical development of cybercities within a new 15x50km "corridor", provision of an advanced telecommunications infrastructure, enactment of an up-to-date legislative framework for the information age and the provision of a set of financial and non-financial incentives. These elements of the ideal multimedia environment and incentives are succinctly captured in a Bill of Guarantees provided by the government to investors. To promote the application of ICT, seven large-scale Flagship Applications were launched. These are Smart Schools, Multi-purpose Card, Telemedicine, Electronic Government, Research and Development Cluster, Borderless Marketing and World-wide Manufacturing Web. Other elements of the MSC include:

- development of an e-Village to promote creative multimedia content development, animation, production and post-production activities.
- a package of incentives, including venture capital, R&D grant, incubator, market access, and human resource development programmes to promote technopreneurship and skills; and
- the Multimedia Development Corporation (MDC) as a high-powered, one-stop super-agency to implement the MSC.

In addition, it is recognised that a well-educated, "knowledge-based" workforce is the most important resource in the new economy. The only way to create this workforce is to invest in education. Malaysia needs to improve basic education for her children, and make advanced education more widely available if she hopes to sustain social transformation and new economic growth. Education is the only means to reduce digital divide and social disparity. To achieve this objective, MSC-status incentives are provided to both public and private institutions of higher learning to accelerate the education and training of human resources for the ICT industry. Tertiary education programmes in ICT have been greatly expanded to meet the demand of the industry. At the primary and the secondary school levels, besides the pilot implementation of the Smart School Flagship Application in 90 schools, the Ministry of Education has embarked on a programme to introduce computers to more than 2,000 schools throughout the country. Skills upgrading of the workforce is also underway. For the civil service, the government has started computer literacy courses for the 850,000 public sector employees. At the same time, the Ministry of Human Resources is providing incentives for the private sector to upgrade the skills of their workforce to meet the challenges of the knowledge economy.

CONCLUSION

The tasks to increase investment in knowledge-based economic activity and to equip the workforce with new skills require time, resources, and sustained efforts by the private sector and the government.

The MSC is a strategic initiative that requires the continuous commitment and active participation of every sector of the economy. The stakes are high, but the cost of not doing it is even higher. For example, if Malaysia does not invest now in information infrastructure and get businesses to adopt electronic commerce, the potential cost to the economy could be very high. While some companies may choose not to transform or re-engineer themselves, their competitors may position themselves to be more cost-effective and more efficient, thus commanding better access to major customers through better utilisation of ICT. Over a period of time, companies that have not transformed will lose their international competitiveness and may become losers in the new economy. However, with supportive government policies, excellent infrastructure and modern telecommunication networks that are put to productive use, entrepreneurship and determination, Malaysia will be in a much better position to reap the benefits of ICT as well as to meet the challenges of the new millennium.

In view of Malaysia's dependency on international trade, the country has no choice but to pursue strategies of creating value in the networked economy. However, in the final analysis, the marketplace rewards the creative and innovative enterprise that commands the knowledge and information to manage the uncertainties.

Internet Strategy

Rising to the Net Challenge

Tan Sri Francis Yeoh
Managing Director
YTL Corporation Bhd

Over the past decade, the Internet has grown by leaps and bounds and spread its web all over the world.

The pervasiveness of the Internet is partly due to its ease of use and transparency. It is an integrator that allows information to be centrally transmitted on a network in either a wired or wireless platform. As a medium, the Internet will be successful because it is an open technology, open business model and open architecture. This openness promotes competition and innovation.

The Internet's openness has also spilled over to online trade or e-commerce. The new economy, or the "nude" economy, is more transparent and exposed compared to the old-style economy, thanks to the Net. Information is no longer the purview of the few as content providers provide ample information for all who access the World Wide Web.

Although it only accounts for a tiny portion of the world economy at present, the emerging e-economy is poised to grow tremendously over the next few years. Such growth, of course, has come about thanks to easy Internet access. Worldwide, wired

Internet users are forecast to grow from 140 million in 1999 to over 320 million by 2002 with over 50 million users located in Asia.

Likewise, e-commerce is poised to see similar meteoric growth. The e-commerce industry recorded billings of US$74 billion in 1999 and this is projected to grow to over US$700 billion by 2003.

In 1999, B2B (business to business) companies took the lion's share with US$59 billion, and this will grow to almost US$600 billion by 2003, five to six times the transacted value projected for B2C (business to consumer) commerce.

By lowering interaction costs and increasing returns and economies of scope and scale in businesses, these forces are streamlining industry supply chains, cutting transaction costs and more importantly, driving the shift of power from the sellers of goods and services to their customers.

THE NEW LANDSCAPE

However, the implementation of e-commerce is not simply a question of automating existing channels and processes. It is a whole new way of doing business.

In general, e-business evolves in three distinct waves, and each wave is characterised by its impact on different growth cycles of the enterprise.

In the first wave, the development of electronic brochureware, portals, and co-branded websites are directed at improving operational efficiency and enhancing near-term performance.

For sustained enhanced performance, the enterprise needs to move to the second wave to expand its range of products and services and regional and global reach. The deliverables include improving customer access, service delivery and customer relations while concurrently providing value to customers with better products and innovative services.

In the third and final wave, the enterprise has to reinvent itself with offerings of new products and services, brand and image reinforcement and rewriting of a new business model to incorporate the 3Cs of communication, commerce and content.

In this new industry landscape, the power is changing hands from sellers of goods and services to consumers who are empowered to trade with suppliers offering the best deals. As supply chains are compressed, services that were once bundled to add value to the chain are being broken up.

For example, in banking services, a transfer between bank accounts costs over US$1.27 if done by a teller, 80% less if transacted via a cash machine and less than 1% of the teller's cost over the Internet. Products are now being bought and sold as commodities on the Net in auctions, reverse auctions and tenders. The Net cuts through all national boundaries and the products and service offerings available on the Net are limitless.

With WAP (Wireless Application Protocol) being carried on cellular networks underscored by 3G introduction, information is freed from its dependence on traditional wired transmission and released from specific backbone networks and markets.

The role of intermediaries is marginalised and their survival is predicated on finding new value-added services in the supply chain. The longer the supply chain, the bigger the opportunities for e-commerce, and the more likely that a business can be disintermediated. The Net is the greatest cost buster ever for industry and end-users. Traditionally, Asian business has an incipiently long supply chain with the attendant pain of dealing with intermediaries at increased cost. Thus, Asian businesses are especially vulnerable to disintermediation via the Net.

Traditional and Net-Generation Companies in the E-Economy

The foundational values of the old economy companies are based on increasing return on investment, cost reductions and customer service in its drive towards higher efficiency and cost-effective operations. With the Internet, values have changed. Innovation and creativity in the field of knowing the customer wins out. As more customers transact over the Net, a strong brand and good customer relationships grow in importance. In the new era, customer relations management and strong branding are vital for survival.

With the advent of e-commerce, the battleground for businesses moves above the e-line. This will see the rise of Net-generation companies. The focus is now on changing industry and market practices to one of innovation. Technology improves the price-to-performance ratios and increases the range of products and services.

The Net-generation companies will improve both the top line and the bottom line.

However, old-economy companies have the advantage of money. When they wake up to the realities of the new economy, they have the money to invest in e-commerce. In no time at all, they can become second to none. The old-economy companies that cease to change will face great problems.

The Way Forward for YTL

Although it is an old-economy company dealing with infrastructure development, with businesses in construction, cement, power, property, and hotels, YTL is embracing e-commerce intensively. With the advantage of 45 years of experience in engineering, property-related activities and power generation, YTL is well-positioned to adopt an Internet strategy that not only leverages on its ever-growing customer base of 500,000, but also its resourceful human capital of about 2000 staff. Exploiting the advantages of the Internet is particularly crucial for YTL if it is to maintain its record of growing its earnings by 33% per annum over the last ten years.

In e-commerce, YTL intends to enjoy first-mover advantage. This is in line with an enviable record where YTL has achieved many firsts and innovations in Malaysia. This includes being the first company to introduce turnkey construction, the first independent power producer (IPP), the first Asian IPP to use non-US$ financing, the first Asian company to issue a "zero coupon" Euro-Convertible Bond and the first non-Japanese Asian company to list on the Tokyo Stock Exchange. In the mid-1990s, YTL successfully and profitably executed an old-economy cement "portal" by suppressing the supply chain through direct import and marketing over one million tonnes of cement, two years prior to the commissioning of YTL's Pahang cement plant. This move was made possible due to the inefficiency of existing suppliers in responding speedily to customers' needs.

Elsewhere, YTL e-Solutions Sdn Bhd was set up with the motto "Empowering Excellence" and an initial paid-up capital of RM100 million to spearhead the Group's Internet initiatives and oversee the transformation of the Group from an Old Economy business to a New Economy compliant "click and brick" enterprise. Discussions are now ongoing to list this vehicle on MESDAQ.

Simultaneously, YTL has also set up an Internet Competency Centre (ICC) comprising 50 knowledge workers with a growing workforce over the next 12 months. The ICC will act as a test-bed for new technologies still being researched and developed and as a training base for interns and YTL employees. To maintain the cutting edge of technical excellence, it has forged alliances with strategic technology partners, Siemens Information and Communication Group and Oracle Systems. These technology partners will advise on system integration and developing a secure, scalable backbone infrastructure configured to handle 100,000 concurrent user sessions.

YTL has acquired a 15% stake in PropertyNetAsia.com, a pan-Asian property e-commerce portal, a multi-listing service company for Asian properties with e-commerce enabling capabilities. The operating company, Grierson, also has a joint venture in Malaysia in which YTL e-Solutions owns 60% equity to develop PropertyNetAsia.com.my. This portal will enable online transactions of RM8 billion worth of YTL's new developments over the next 5 years. YTL has also rolled out the YTL Community super portal which contains online functionalities including e-learning, auction, games, property, news, travel and the BintangWalk.com, a website showcasing the Ritz-Carlton, JW Marriott, Lot 10, Starhill and a host of restaurants and eateries in the prime Bintang Walk precinct. Features offered include real-time online bookings of hotel rooms, restaurants, and a shopping cart offering best buys from merchants, packaged and delivered anywhere at competitive rates.

With the convergence of all these efforts, YTL hopes to build its own online community of loyal customers. YTL will offer premium services to this community in order to increase the "stickiness" of these customer relationships. This community also offers YTL a golden opportunity to cross-sell its range of complementary product and service offerings.

In short, we welcome the Internet revolution. WWW is not a three-letter acronym for What Went Wrong. The challenge is to turn your whole outfit from a potential dinosaur into a dynamo.

Industry

Agriculture

Reaping Rich Harvests from Innovation

Datuk Dr Effendi Norwawi
Minister, Ministry of Agriculture

The organisational challenge of the Ministry of Agriculture (MOA) is to determine the most effective mechanism to carry out its functions to transform the agriculture sector during the Third National Agricultural Policy (NAP3) period. The NAP3, which covers the period 1998 to 2010, seeks to provide the gradual but effective transformation of the agricultural and forestry sectors as Malaysia moves into the new millennium. The Policy incorporates several new strategies to deal with the expected challenges and changes to the international economy and addresses a number of national concerns related to agricultural development and the economy as a whole. These concerns are enhancing food security and combating inflation, increasing productivity, promoting private sector investment in agriculture, enhancing exports and reducing imports and encouraging conservation and sustainable use of natural resources.

MOA's functions are to find practical technological and marketing solutions to address these national concerns. The vision of MOA is to ensure that the country continues to be a world leader in the area of agricultural research and production of tropical products, developing state-of-the-art technologies and information systems for production, post-harvest handling, processing and distribution, to support the cluster development of the agricultural industries as envisaged in the IMP1 (Industrial Master Plan 1) and NAP3.

Some basic questions have to be answered immediately, such as, "With globalisation, liberalisation, and the New Economy, what lies ahead for the agriculture sector?

What kind of agricultural products will be the winners? Who are the players in the agriculture sector and the environment in which they operate?" To find the answers to these questions, we have to deal with the exogenous factors of competition and complexity, e-commerce, the Internet and industry structuring and restructuring, the endogenous human factor and corporate culture. Globalisation and e-commerce will significantly change the operations of the business environment. Familiar marketplaces are becoming increasingly complex and the traditional rules of conducting business are no longer relevant. With the eventual dissolution of trade barriers under the World Trade Organisation and the Asean Free Trade Area, players in the sector will have little choice but to compete within a larger market. The players need to be proactive participants in the new economy, seeking out opportunities to gain strong footholds in a business environment that continues to evolve.

The focus of development is on the players in the transformation process. In this process, apart from technology development, we have to focus on the application of scientific knowledge in the form of "information-intensive technology" at the farm and factory levels, and this will represent a major challenge in the process of implementing the NAP3. The new mechanism must recognise the importance of technology transfer process. The frontier of technology is always the human frontier. It is the combination of science and human emotion for successful technology utilisation. It's a very, very rare skill to be able to bring these two together. That's why there have been so many instances where technology has seemed so attractive but failed completely.

In the transformation process, we have to explore ideas that are beyond traditional agriculture and conventional technologies. In this regard, we have to examine the opportunities arising from the development of biology and information sciences. Recent developments have shown that the merging between the two sciences is where wealth will be generated. Entrepreneurs are using the emerging enabling technologies/tools of computers, web-based technologies, robotics, nanotechnology, spectroscopy, bioinformatics, biotechnology and transgenic technologies, to develop new products and services in the healthcare, food and agriculture, chemical and material industries.

This group of entrepreneurs is a new breed who are highly educated (PhDs), have spent the earlier part of their careers in research institutions and have the imagination and the foresight to use these converging technologies developed by public research institutions to develop commercial products and services and create wealth in the process. The focus of product development is on natural products discovery, healthcare, food and agriculture. The explosive growth and far-reaching influence of the Web and Internet communications are rapidly changing every aspect of healthcare, food and agriculture, chemical and material industries.

Specialised companies have evolved to provide services which will speed up the process of natural products discovery, healthcare and food products development and commercialisation. These are mainly bioinformatics companies developing software and Internet-based technologies that allow for management of large volumes of data, including electronic data capturing, monitoring and analysis, and decision-making.

Strategic alliances or collaborations or value-added partnerships are common for business development and technology transfer especially between specialised companies with patented technologies in the natural products discovery, healthcare and food products development and commercialisation process. In fact, alliances and partnerships are reshaping the life science industry. It has become a more intelligent way of doing business. Since 1978, there are more than 8,000 alliances in the life science industry. These alliances include a biotechnology company partnering with a major drug company (drug/biotech), a university (university/biotech) or another biotechnology company.

Outsourcing has become a major strategy for natural products discovery and development. The specialised companies such as Contract Research Organisations offering research services, Contract Packers and Manufacturers and consulting companies offering legal and regulatory affairs services have become an important component of the industry structure. Contract manufacturing has become an important strategic tool of genomics and natural products companies.

"What you know" is becoming more important in the New Economy. There is a need to build partnerships and strategic alliances between our research organisations and their clientele. Technology prospecting should be a new strategic tool of our research organisations to serve their clientele. Ideas from technology prospecting can be translated into new products and services fast enough to stay on the edge of the innovation curve. These partnerships and strategic alliances can continually connect people with good ideas and test the changing market, always searching for the next innovation. We must remember that players in the sector have to respond to the tremendous opportunities opened up by the development of e-commerce which has enabled producers to reach out to global suppliers and markets at lower cost and connect with their customers. There is a need to concentrate on the core businesses in which the clientele has a competitive advantage. This is to survive the increasingly fierce onslaught of competition from abroad as markets are further opened in Asia.

We have to change radically and adopt strategic thinking, especially the effective management of human capital, to meet the challenges posed by globalisation, liberalisation, e-commerce and biotechnology. The main message is to commence the transformation process now. We have to respond quickly to the needs of the markets. The New Economy is based on speed and it operates on "Internet time" and responds more quickly to economic, technological and market changes. These changes generate a lot of information and the scale, complexity and greater quantities of information impose even stronger demands on our capabilities to deliver and serve our markets.

There is also a need to win the war for talent in the tight labour market. Market-transforming forces, ranging from globalisation, e-commerce and biotechnology, will produce a dramatic increase in the number of different skills required to propel our industries successfully into the future. These talents include flexibility, innovation and rapid, high-quality decision-making. The leadership has to be fast and flexible enough to deal with varying crises and able to manage teams of executives with diverse talents. Such leadership must be able to provide solid management with decisions focused on quality of assets (knowledge capital and talent), innovation and value creation.

The skills required for the development and utilisation of the above new technologies are in computational biology, bioinformatics, automation engineering, software engineering, project leadership, business development and technology transfer to clients. There is a need for the players in the sector to acquire the technical skills in computer science, automation and robotics, biostatistics, bioinformatics, chemoinformatics, etc. along with soft skills in team orientation, customer focus, communication and leadership. It is thus important to have an effective human development programme as well as an attractive service scheme to retain talented and skilled workers in the sector.

The aim is for the sector to move into new frontier technologies and business development in food and agriculture industries within 10 years. The challenges will involve research, technology development, transfer and commercialisation, information management and IT infrastructure and business reorientation for a more integrated development of a modern, dynamic and competitive food and agriculture sector.

Tourism

Making Malaysia a top Tourist Destination

Dato' Abdul Kadir Sheikh Fadzir
Minister, Ministry of Culture, Arts & Tourism

Tourism has been identified as a key subsector of the services sector in generating foreign exchange earnings for the country. The growth of this sector during the period 1990-1996 was commendable. It culminated in tourism receipts of RM10.35 billion in 1996, making this sector the second largest foreign exchange earner for the country after manufacturing.

1997-1998 was a difficult year for the tourism industry in Malaysia. The weak performance of the industry stemmed from a few unfortunate events that shaped the scenario for this period. A spate of negative reports in the international media on haze pollution, outbreaks of coxsackie virus, Japanese encephalitis and cholera and the currency crisis in the Asian region adversely affected the tourism industry. The number of tourist arrivals in 1997 thus declined by 13% to 6.21 million and tourism receipts dipped 6.3% to RM 9.70 billion.

The downturn in business for tour agencies, airlines and the hotel industry due to the drop in tourist arrivals affected retail trade, restaurants as well as other service providers relevant to the industry.

INBOUND TOURISM

The country's main objective for tourism is to increase the number of international visitors to Malaysia. Malaysia has consistently registered arrival figures exceeding 7 million tourists since 1994 with the exception of 1997 and 1998, when the numbers dipped to 6.2 million and 5.55 million respectively, as a direct result of the Asian financial crisis. However, the arrival figure for 1999 was 7.93 million, thus surpassing the previous high of 7.47 million achieved in 1995.

The arrivals for 1999 reflected a rebound which was consistent with the economic recovery being experienced in the region. Singaporeans still constitute more than half of the total market although the trend appears to be decreasing as arrivals from other markets gradually increased over the years.

TOURISM RECEIPTS

The second objective is to increase revenue from tourism, largely by promoting longer average length of stay and emphasising more quality tourists.

Tourism receipts, with the exception of the 1997-1998 period, have been gradually on the rise since 1994. The 1999 receipts of RM12.32 billion represented a substantial increase over 1998's tourism receipts of RM8.58 billion. The higher than expected revenue in 1999 could be attributed to the increase in arrival numbers as the average per diem expenditure of tourists remained unchanged. To a significant extent, it could be due to tourists taking full advantage of the depreciation of the ringgit with Malaysia regarded as a top value-for-money destination.

DOMESTIC TOURISM

The growth of the local tourism sector parallels the rise of the international tourism business in Malaysia. A study on domestic tourism by a local university revealed that up to 13.8 million trips were made by Malaysians within the country in 1997. Forecasts were also undertaken which showed an upward trend. By the year 2000, it was forecast that 15.1 million trips would be made by the local population to various destinations within the country. Among the measures, the additional Saturday holidays would help to further boost domestic tourism.

In addition, with the depreciation of the local currency and relatively smaller disposable incomes, generally fewer Malaysians would be travelling abroad for leisure. This provides opportunities to further boost domestic tourism.

MICE MARKETS

The Meetings, Incentives, Conventions and Exhibitions (MICE) market has been identified as a significant niche for Malaysia's tourism industry in the long term. Its expansion over the years has been encouraging and it was the only segment virtually unaffected by the regional crisis.

There was a 150% jump in the number of conventions from 393 in 1992 to 800 in 1998, while the number of participants increased from 174,267 to 300,036 during the same period. Correspondingly, the total expenditure in the MICE segment rose from RM551.2 million in 1992 to RM990.1 million in 1998. In effect, the local MICE segment is experiencing faster growth than its international counterpart and this certainly helps fill the vacuum during hard times when international meetings are not easy to come by.

HOTEL INDUSTRY

The hotel industry, which developed at a rapid pace during the last decade or so, is currently facing a temporary oversupply of rooms. This is largely due to the retardation in regional travel resulting from the economic crisis and, to a certain extent, the political uncertainties in the region as perceived by long haul travellers.

In 1997, the number of hotels increased to 1,365, breaching the earlier target set under the Seventh Malaysia Plan of 1,340 hotels by year 2000. Consequently, there will be a long lapse of time before investment in this sector returns to the previous levels, arising from the prevailing overcapacity.

The average occupancy rate, an indicator of hotel business, declined as a direct consequence of the crisis. The overall hotel average occupancy level which peaked in 1995 at 65.5% dropped to a new low of 49.9% in 1998. A slight recovery was recorded for 1999 at 51.7%.

AIR ACCESSIBILITY

Air access into Malaysia, in terms of flight frequency and seat capacity, expanded from 725 international flights and 146,879 seats weekly in 1994 to a high of 1,058 flights and 228,409 seats weekly in 1997. As a result of the crisis, international flights dipped 16.4% to 899 while capacity also fell to 207,256 seats weekly in 1998. In 1999, the numbers improved marginally to 908 flights and 207,554 seats weekly.

ISSUES AND CHALLENGES

The Malaysian tourism industry is currently at a crossroads. The setback experienced during the recent economic crisis apparently warranted some rethinking and careful re-evaluation of how the industry could be better managed and manoeuvred.

Our target is to ensure that tourist arrivals will increase at an average of 6.9% per annum to reach 14.3 million tourists by 2005 as compared to the pre-crisis growth of about 10%. To address the situation, a more strategic framework for tourism promotion is needed, taking into consideration the following issues and challenges facing the industry.

ESTABLISHING AND DEVELOPING TOURISM BRAND POSITIONING IN KEY MARKETS OVERSEAS

There is a need for effective branding to reposition Malaysia as a top-of-mind destination in both regional and international markets, due to intense competitiveness in the region. As such, a compendious caption or identity should be formulated as an exquisite yet captivating master brand. The brand shall be part of the long-term image-building process to position the nation in the international travel arena. In retrospect, the brand chosen for the country previously, i.e. "Fascinating Malaysia" in 1990 and "Malaysia Fascinating Destination" in 1994 could not be sustained with the advent of the new era.

"Malaysia Truly Asia," the new brand chosen for Malaysia, was launched in late 1999. This brand reflects the distinct cultural diversity of the country as Malaysia is a microcosm of Asia, having a unique culture interwoven with those of major Asian civilisations from India, China and the Malay archipelago.

This brand is expected to create a universal label which is easily recognisable and forms the hallmark of Malaysia. It is to be used in all marketing and promotional undertakings by both the public and private sectors. Additionally, it is expected to readily elicit recall in particular by repeat customers and this may influence their decision on the choice of destination.

In the interests of all concerned, it is best that all public and private agencies involved in the tourism business integrate the brand into all their promotional products, advertising and public relations activities.

MANAGING TOURISM PRODUCTS AND DEVELOPMENT

The tourism sector is increasingly becoming more competitive. For sustainable tourism, promotions and marketing must take cognisance of the needs, tastes and preferences of visitors from different countries and regions because of varied consumer demands.

Focused promotions are to be carried out in strategic markets such as Hong Kong, Taiwan, India and the Middle East as well as Australia, Europe and the United States. These markets are not affected by the economic downturn. Unique selling points are nature, sports, culture and heritage while bearing in mind that shopping and MICE need to be aggressively marketed.

ADEQUATE AIR ACCESS TO DIVERSIFY TOURISM MARKETS

Although most of the tourists come principally from Singapore (60%) and Thailand (7%) overland, adequate air access from other countries must be exploited, especially with the Government's policy to diversify our tourism markets.

To diversify the tourist markets and reduce overdependence on the Singapore and Thai markets:

a) MAS needs to negotiate more aggressively and expand international air access especially in new tourist-generating markets such as the Middle East, India and China;
b) it may be necessary to consider paying a higher royalty for landing rights in new markets such as India as the net gain to the nation is likely to be many times more; and
c) we must strive to make the Kuala Lumpur International Airport a new regional hub.

While adequate and consistent budgets must be made available on a continuous basis, more important is the effective utilisation of resources to achieve the goals of increased tourist arrivals and receipts. These include:

a) adequate planning in promotional efforts because timing of promotions in overseas markets must be planned as holiday packages are usually booked a year or so in advance;
b) greater strength and depth in strategic planning and marketing; and
c) more utilisation of Internet facilities by creating up-to-date websites.

ENHANCEMENT, PRESERVATION AND CONSERVATION OF SUSTAINABLE TOURISM DEVELOPMENT

Malaysia is fortunate to have been endowed with so many tourist resources and attractions to suit the tastes and preferences of every visitor to the country. One of Malaysia's main tourist draws is nature-based products. As such, eco-tourism and sustainable development are significant areas that merit due consideration when drawing up tourism masterplans and promotions. In this regard, reference must be made to the National Eco-Tourism Plan when planning nature-based projects. The National Eco-Tourism Plan was drawn up by The World Wide Fund for Nature (WWF) Malaysia to assist the Government at both Federal and State level in the development and management of Malaysia's eco-tourism products.

MALAYSIA AS A SHOPPING DESTINATION

The issue for Malaysia would be how best to get tourists to do more shopping in Malaysia. In line with this, positioning Malaysia as a shopping haven would require more aggressive efforts to promote and advertise Malaysia with emphasis on the duty-free tax-exempt status of a wide range of consumer products. In addition, the availability of the latest fashions, as well as a range of designer goods, is crucial in making Malaysia a distribution centre for branded goods and accessories.

PROMOTION OF MICE AS AN INDUSTRY

This segment represents the upmarket or the high yield tourist market. The expenditure pattern of this segment could provide much higher and faster revenue for the host country. Bidding for and hosting international conventions and prestigious events such as Formula One is an effective way of boosting tourism income for Malaysia. In the light of increasing regional competition, efforts must be intensified and serious attention be given to the quality of facilities and services often required for international MICE events.

For long-term planning, a new mechanism along similar lines of action taken by our neighbouring countries for strengthening Tourism Malaysia's MICE division needs to be considered. This would imply giving serious attention to the quality of facilities by encouraging the installation of state-of-the-art technologies to upgrade the existing facilities and services in places where MICE events are often held.

PROMOTING DOMESTIC TOURISM

Promoting Malaysia as an exciting holiday destination to its own citizens is an even more challenging task for tourism agencies, both in the private and public sectors. More effective measures are necessary to inculcate planned holiday habits among Malaysians. Agencies need to develop more affordable, value-for-money packages to encourage domestic travel. This would help offset the low occupancy rate in accommodation-based establishments during low season.

FOSTERING REGIONAL ALLIANCES

Apart from fostering strategic alliances among the airlines, closer rapport among regional bodies and trade intermediaries is necessary to create synergistic benefits through the process of complementing products and services in a conducive customer-friendly business environment.

In addition, more bilateral cooperation with specific markets need to be worked out.

USE OF NEW TECHNOLOGIES

With the advent of the information age, the way business is conducted in the tourism sector is being rapidly transformed.

The Internet offers a cheap and faster mode of communication and this medium calls for different marketing and promotional strategies, which enables up-to-date information to be readily available to potential travellers. Thus, IT and new technologies should form an important and indispensable tool in promotions and marketing, even though traditional methods are still necessary.

Through a strategic framework and linkages, Tourism Malaysia aims to market Malaysia as a top destination and make the industry a major contributor to the nation's socioeconomic development.

Consumer and Intellectual Property

The Way Forward

Tan Sri Muhyiddin Mohd Yassin
Minister, Ministry of Domestic Trade and Consumer Affairs

As economies develop and more countries begin to acquire the use of new technologies, consumerism and intellectual property protection assume a greater sense of urgency. This new awareness becomes acute as nationals of these countries acquire inventive skills and consumer and intellectual property (IP) protection demand higher national priorities. Consumers in developing countries are no longer passive users of inventions from the developed world. National interests are now measured in terms of a Government's ability to safeguard quality and access to goods and services as well as protect the rights of inventors and innovators of new technologies.

Alongside the noble intentions in inventions, new skills and technologies also present opportunities for the unlawful exploitation of intellectual property. This scourge is particularly obvious in the copyright industry where digital technology has rendered copyright infringement immensely rewarding. The relative ease in pirating copyrighted works and the seeming public acquiescence in such activities (as evident in the music and the software industries) present major challenges to authorities of both developed and developing countries. Malaysia, in its effort to be the regional hub of the IT industry, is concerned about of this problem and will no doubt take measures to address it. This will pave the way for a conducive environment for the development of the Multimedia Super Corridor.

Efforts to improve consumer and IP protection must necessarily relate to the:

1. Enhancement of public awareness
2. Provisions for adequate facilities and references
3. Reviewing and updating of IP laws
4. Effective enforcement of IP laws, and
5. International involvement and networking

Public outreach programmes undertaken to enhance awareness on IP matters include talks over the mass media and road shows in the form of seminars and workshops throughout the country where basic information on IP references, legal rights and protection, and incentives in terms of awards and recognition to investors can be disseminated.

The IP Office, through the Intellectual Property Training Centre, undertakes specialised exposure programmes for selected target groups like judges, public prosecutors, enforcement officers, IP practitioners, entrepreneurs and students. These exposure programmes have the support and cooperation of business chambers, the Malaysian Intellectual Property Association, relevant Ministries, universities, research institutions, the World Intellectual Property Organisation, the European Patent Office and other foreign Governments' IP bodies.

With the vision to make the country's IP Office into the region's IP centre, current efforts in the automation of IP records and management will undergo continuous enhancement and upgrading. Facilities for research and exploitation of inventions will be upgraded to accommodate the increasing number of researchers and inventors in the country.

Adequate consumer and IP rights protection requires the judicious reviewing and updating of relevant laws and regulations. Recent amendments to IP laws and regulations, though primarily meant to fulfil Malaysia's obligations to the Agreement on Trade-Related Aspects of Intellectual Property Rights (TRIPS), also introduced new provisions to enhance rights and protection, both for the users and owners of intellectual properties.

In Malaysia, consumer and IP protection rates high on the Government's agenda. This is noticeable from the enactment of the Trade Description Act 1972 (TDA), the Optical Disc Act 2000 and the recent setting up of the Special Copyright Task Force and Copyright Tribunal. More often than not, the Trade Description Act provides expedient judicial means of dispensing with intellectual property infringement cases. Similarly, the Optical Disc Act is expected to curb at source the unbridled activities of optical disc manufacturers, said to be responsible for putting Malaysia on the world map of copyright piracy. The Copyright Tribunal arbitrates disputes arising from the legal claims of copyright owners and the users of the copyright works.

Existing IP laws and regulations offer little protection without enforcement. In Malaysia, preventive measures such as raids and seizures on offending parties continue and are often conducted repeatedly since most owners of infringed products feel that it is more expedient to rely on short-term preventive measures rather than seek remedies through the court.

IP rights and protection transcend national boundaries. The way forward must be paved with the required national infrastructure, as well as global positioning characterised by active involvement in, and networking with international IP bodies. Our participation is crucial, as evident in the current excitement over the need to convene a new round of talks among World Trade Organisation member countries, particularly by developed countries, despite resistance from most developing countries. Many issues, including the patenting of indigenous common knowledge by multinational corporations, are seen as unfairly skewed against developing countries. There is therefore a growing concern that this form of monopoly would increase the cost of imports and technologies, and thus widen the gap between the developed and developing countries.

For a country like Malaysia, consumer and IP protection can no longer be viewed in terms of owner/user situations, since more Malaysian nationals are also IP rights owners now. In fact, the current concern over the counterfeiting of goods and copyright piracy in the music and film industries is symptomatic of the need to address the problem in a more equitable manner. A stronger legal, judicial and enforcement infrastructure must be in place to ensure reasonable public access to commercialised creations while providing a conducive environment for inventions and exploitations.

Education

Sowing the Seeds of Great Minds

Tan Sri Musa Mohamad
Minister, Ministry of Education

Malaysia has done remarkably well over the last few decades and all indications suggest optimism in our continuing ability to advance into the ranks of developed nations. We look at the 21st century as a time of new challenges and a time for new resolve. There are powerful dynamics reshaping Malaysian education, and technology is very much at the heart of this transformation. How we educate the minds of young Malaysians and shape their values now will go a long way towards defining the destiny of this nation in the years to come.

The critical factors of economic growth such as capital, natural resources and cheap labour have been in our favour. For us to continue enjoying the fruits of our country's economic growth, we must face the challenges of sustainability in an increasingly globalised world. In this regard, we have reached the point in our development process where we can begin to identify human talents as the critical resource to take us further. Our economic growth is dependent on the availability of an educated workforce, which will have to be increasingly multi-skilled, innovative and creative, versatile and adaptable. Malaysia's passage towards development will rely more and more on knowledge workers, particularly in technological fields, and will depend more and more on an increasing pool of leaders and entrepreneurs to pave the way. It is in this direction that our national human capital formation should move in the future.

As evidenced by recent key policy decisions, education in our country is being liberalised, and rightly so, as educational achievement is the cornerstone from which national prosperity can be constructed. Our education system should have the capacity to make available an educated workforce of skilled and competent individuals. At the top of the educational pyramid, given the existence of these basic talents, should appear the creatively gifted, the "great minds." They should be able to utilise their dreams and ideas to discover and create what does not yet exist, be it in the arts, the sciences or technology.

Fundamental to this realisation are educational inputs and reforms, which must be introduced to ensure that no child should be left behind. No child should be allowed to miss school or to drift through school. No effort should be spared to detect, tap, nurture and cultivate the talents that are the future "great minds" among us. What we should seek is a democracy of educational excellence for all our young people through the 21st century. We need a new resolve to meet the many challenges before us and we have to put aside all the issues that impair our educational growth.

Our hope for the future surely begins by keeping a strong focus on the early years of childhood and schooling when the minds of our children are just sparking. To ensure a quality primary and secondary education for all our young from which would spring forth the intelligent elite, we must work hard towards elevating the teaching profession. We have to give teachers and principals the resources they need and free up their creativity to achieve results and reach high standards. We must make sweeping efforts to make teaching a first-class profession. The next generation of principals must be created based on competence, ability and personality.

We have to make efforts to turn around under-performing schools where the basics of education must be mastered. Our children must have a strong foundation in mathematics, science and technology, acquired in what should be the modern classrooms of the 21st century.

Vocational and technical studies need to be accorded better emphasis and higher status as well as be developed as alternative avenues for those students who excel in "hands-on" applications.

Higher education should in turn allow for the fusion of the arts, sciences and technology that would enable young talents to acquire specialised knowledge and skills and be knowledge workers of the future, and yet be well-grounded in inter-disciplinary and multi-disciplinary pursuits. Democratisation in higher education should be the ideal with public and private sector institutions providing universal access to formal and informal higher education through conventional and unconventional means, including e-learning. No qualified child would be turned away due to financial constraints. Research and post-graduate education should also occupy centre stage with young talents, particularly among the faculty, encouraged to research at the frontiers of knowledge and innovation.

Keeping 'great minds' is as important as creating and nurturing them. Globalisation will make it even more difficult to keep them particularly in fields where good talents are scarce. We need, therefore, to do much more to keep our 'great minds' home and contributing to the wellbeing of our nation.

The 21st century will pose new challenges to a developing nation such as ours. In this new millennium we have to guard ourselves against being vulnerable and to remain at the cutting edge of technology. For this, we need an army of "great minds" which we have to nurture right now, if not, we will be swallowed up by the tide of globalisation. Our educational reforms must be potent enough to sow the seeds of "great minds" and this can only be accomplished with the cooperation of all stakeholders including parents and the community at large.

Health

Enhancing the Nation's Well-being

Dato' Chua Jui Meng
Minister, Ministry of Health

Malaysians have every reason to be proud of the achievements that we have made in health since Independence. Life expectancy at birth, which stood at 55.8 years for males and 58.2 years for females in 1957, had risen to 69.9 years for males and 74.9 years for females by 1999. High maternal, infant, and toddler mortality rates, which were at 2.8 per 1,000 live-births, 73.0 per 1,000 live-births and 8.9 per 1,000 toddlers respectively at the time of Independence, had been brought down to 0.2, 7.9 and 0.6 per thousand by 1999.

Through good planning and sagacious investment in a series of 5-year development plans, the number of public health facilities in the country had increased from a mere 66 hospitals and a sprinkling of sanitary boards at the time of Independence, to an impressive network of 120 hospitals, 128 health offices, 773 health clinics, 1,990 community clinics and 107 Maternal and Child Health clinics under the Ministry of Health alone by 1999. This network provides all levels of promotional, preventive, curative and rehabilitative healthcare to an estimated population of 22.7 million.

In fact, as early as 1996, the 2nd National Health and Morbidity Survey conducted by the Ministry of Health showed that 88.5% of the population already lived within 5km of a static health facility, while the more remote areas of the country were well served by no less than 194 mobile clinics of all sorts, indicating the high degree of accessibility to healthcare enjoyed by the population.

While those who can afford it may turn to the private sector, attracted by the perception of better quality care, more amenities and shorter queues (at the 225 private hospitals and a few thousand private clinics throughout the country in 1999), the majority of the population can still fall back readily on the highly subsidised public healthcare system which spent up to RM4.5 billion or 6.1% of the total federal government expenditure in 1999. This makes the latter one of the most affordable public healthcare systems in the region, if not the world. Indeed, few countries in the world can boast of such commendable achievements in so short a time.

VISION FOR HEALTH

As we forge ahead towards developed nation status by 2020, we will continue to be guided by our Vision for Health, which states that:

"Malaysia is to be a nation of healthy individuals, families and communities, through a health system that is equitable, affordable, efficient, technologically appropriate, environmentally adaptable and consumer-friendly, with emphasis on quality, innovation, health promotion and respect for human dignity, and which promotes individual responsibility and community participation towards an enhanced quality of life."

In partnership with all stakeholders in health, the Ministry of Health will continue to facilitate and support the people in attaining their full potential in health, motivating them to appreciate health as a valuable asset, and taking positive actions to improve further and sustain their health status, so that they may be socially and economically productive and enjoy an enhanced quality of life.

FROM INDUSTRIAL AGE MEDICINE TO INFORMATION AGE HEALTHCARE

In tandem with the switch from a production-based economy to a knowledge-based economy as we move into the new century, the Ministry of Health is poised to exploit the full potential of cutting-edge information and multimedia technologies in transforming its healthcare delivery system to further improve health outcomes.

Riding on the Multimedia Super Corridor Infrastructure which had cost the government RM14 billion to set up in the last 5 years, Malaysia's Telemedicine (or Telehealth) Blueprint will provide the framework for the whole nation to leapfrog from industrial age medicine to information age healthcare.

Defined as "the integration of information technologies, telecommunication technologies, human-machine interface technologies and health technologies to deliver healthcare and to promote the health status of the people," telehealth will be the key enabler in the 21st century. Telehealth will provide the population with an accessible, integrated, high-quality, effective, efficient and affordable healthcare system that will be regarded as one of the best in the world and will link Malaysia to the global network of virtual health services.

The focus of this new healthcare system will be on people and services. Individuals and families will be empowered to play the major role in managing their own health through appropriate and timely knowledge transfer. The key emphasis will be on wellness. Services, resources and technologies will be structured to empower and enable people to maintain the highest possible state of health and wellbeing throughout their lives.

THE TELEHEALTH PILOT PROJECTS

For a start, four high-impact pilot projects, which are presently in the final stages of development, will provide the springboard for the national roll-out of telehealth. These are:

i. Massed Customised/Personalised Health Information and Education (MCPHIE);
ii. Continuing Medical Education (CME);
iii. Teleconsultation; and
iv. Lifetime Health Plan (LHP).

MCPHIE is about creating and delivering network-based high quality, customised and personalised health information and education content to individuals at home or close to home, thus empowering and encouraging them to take responsibility for their own health.

CME will be provided through distance learning methods to all healthcare professionals in the country, making available to them knowledge databases, multimedia courseware, interactive training programmes, and electronic textbooks, journals and magazines.

Face-to-face teleconsultation between individuals and/or healthcare providers over a multimedia network, supported by network-linked medical instruments and imaging systems, will enable front-line clinical personnel to deliver high-quality healthcare irrespective of location. Such consultations could be supported by automated care pathways, clinical resource-scheduling systems and clinical decision-support (or expert) systems that will assist clinicians in determining diagnoses, developing treatment regimes and monitoring an individual's progress.

The LHP will provide an individual with lifelong, personalised health management tools to plan and manage his own health, access health services and record details of his health and illnesses. The person's electronic medical records will capture longitudinal views of his interactions with different healthcare providers at different places and at different times. These records will be integrated with a Clinical Support System and an Information Management System to make for a coherent and meaningful personalised life-plan that is secure and allows for easy retrieval, in a seamless continuum of care from womb-to-tomb.

These applications, in particular CME and teleconsultation, are also expected to help reduce healthcare professionals' reluctance to serve in rural areas and smaller towns by providing the means for continuing professional development which are sadly lacking in these areas presently.

THE CHANGE MANAGEMENT PROCESS

The Ministry of Health recognises that the implementation and roll-out of telehealth in Malaysia must be supported by a comprehensive change management process that integrates a number of enabling strategies and activities. Telehealth must be aligned with the national health vision and support national health goals. The organisation of health services needs to be re-designed and processes re-engineered to facilitate computerisation and online delivery, and to ensure that services are effectively integrated, focused on the person and provided at home or close to home.

Hospitals and health clinics in both the public and private sectors nationwide will need to go online in order to promote integrated healthcare. Healthcare providers need to learn and re-learn new skills in managing the new healthcare paradigm. Already we have in place two ultra-modern public hospitals and one health clinic at Selayang and Putrajaya which are paperless and filmless, and several more are in the pipeline. Since 1997, the Ministry has also successfully put in place a nationwide "Virtual Private Network" costing RM12 million, linking all Ministry of Health hospitals, state health departments and health offices. The next phase of this network will extend the linkage to all health clinics and community clinics throughout the country. This network will serve as a suitable platform for the eventual roll-out of telehealth.

The general population needs to be prepared for the major changes linked to telehealth. To ensure equity and avert any digital divide among the population, people who cannot afford their own online connections may access the various telehealth applications, with the assistance of healthcare providers, at the nearest public health facilities.

Thus, through nationwide accessibility to health information and virtual health services, telehealth is poised to dramatically change the way the public and healthcare professionals interact with the healthcare system of the 21st century. People will access healthcare services and manage their personal health in an empowered and knowledge-rich environment, while healthcare professionals will blend this high-tech approach with the high-touch healthcare that they have been traditionally trained to deliver.

It remains to be seen how well the public will accept this new kind of healthcare delivery system, and how well improvements in education and computer literacy will enhance the public's understanding and use of online medical information. Undoubtedly, the affordability and user-friendliness of these technologies will be important, and initially, we will also need to learn the types of medical problems that can be safely handled online.

CONCLUSION

As Malaysia sets in place the building blocks for this new healthcare system of the future, it will take on the role of a leader and an international showcase in healthcare, recognised for its commitment, innovation and ability to enhance the health status of its people by leveraging on the dynamic technologies of the Information Age. It will establish a virtual centre of excellence for telehealth, which will merit international recognition for the products, services and expertise that it offers towards enhancing the nation's health.

Smarter People

Upgrading Malaysia's Human Resources

Datuk Dr Fong Chan Onn
Minister, Ministry of Human Resources

Intellectual capital is the key for economies to gain and retain competitive edge and thereon prosper. As noted in the World Development Report 1999, for countries that are in the vanguard of the world economy, the balance between knowledge and resources has shifted so far towards the former that knowledge has become the most important factor determining the standard of living—more than land, tools or labour. This explains why developed countries can sustain growth whereas developing economies, even those with unlimited labour and ample capital, do not do as well. The world's technologically advanced economies are truly knowledge-based. Knowledge has, therefore, rightly come to be regarded as the basic form of capital. This is the central notion of the knowledge economy.

National economic growth as well as corporate success, then, is driven by the accumulation of knowledge. This is because technology is based on knowledge. Furthermore, any new technological breakthrough, rather than having a one-off impact, can create technical platforms for further innovations. Investment can make technology more valuable and vice-versa. The non-rivalry and technical platform effects of new technology can lead to increasing rather than diminishing returns on technological investment. It is this virtuous circle that can raise a country's growth rate permanently.

A country's capacity to take advantage of the knowledge economy depends on how quickly it can become a 'learning economy'. Learning means not only using new technologies to access global knowledge, but also using them to communicate with other people about innovation. In the learning economy, individuals, firms and countries will be able to create wealth in proportion to their capacity to learn and share innovation. Thus, while Information and Communications Technology (ICT), should not be taken as synonymous with the knowledge economy, it plays a crucial role. ICT is in fact a key enabler for releasing the creative potential and knowledge embodied in people.

In order to make investments in technology, a country must have the required human capital. This intellectual capital is "grown" through education and training. However, to enable people to participate in the rapid process of technological progress, education must become less about passing on information and focus more on teaching people how to learn as well as to think, especially creative thinking. People will have to be proactive, to discover new knowledge and deploy it to create new products or even new industries. People will have to be comfortable and adept in the use of technology. These necessitate, among others, upstream changes in the education and training system.

Education and training must imbue in people the mentality to be open to change, embrace change and view change and future uncertainties as opportunities rather than hurdles. No less important, education and training must look beyond the confines of our own society, and enable people to understand larger trends affecting domestic and international developments. More so than at any other time in history, therefore, education has been thrust to the forefront of responding to the challenges of rapid technological change.

However, instead of a long, continuous process of education before an individual enters the world of work, education and training will have to be a lifelong venture. Formal education before entering the workforce will remain vital to provide the fundamental core skills and knowledge. However, education and training will have to be seen as that full cycle of lifelong and continuous learning. It can no longer be a privilege for the young, but a quest by all. After the traditional formal education stage, it should be available in digestible slices throughout life.

Skill training is widely accessible to Malaysians. The Government is expanding the physical capacity of public sector training institutes and building new ones. By July 2001, the combined capacity of the Industrial Training Institutes (ITIs) and Advanced Technology Centres (ADTECs) under the Ministry of Human Resources is expected to realise a total enrolment of 17,000 full-time trainees. This represents more than a quadrupling of the capacity over the last five years. The expansion is set to continue at no slower pace under the Eighth Malaysia Plan.

It is not merely a numbers game. The ADTECs are a new set of training institutes under the Ministry of Human Resources. While the ITIs have mainly been conducting certificate courses at levels 1-2 of the Malaysian Skill Certificate Scheme, ADTECs' programmes are at the diploma and advanced diploma levels. They are intended to fulfil the need for a particular category of knowledge workers, i.e. the technologists, who are needed to undertake the critical role of knowledge deployment.

The advanced level programmes at the ADTECs are also important in other ways. By establishing a career path for those who opt for careers in the skilled-based occupations, societal perceptions will hopefully change for the positive. More of our young people, with the support of their kin, should be encouraged to undergo training rather than enter the job market without any skills.

The avenue for personal advancement up to the advanced diploma level under the Malaysian Skill Certificate scheme is also designed to encourage Malaysians to upgrade and acquire new skills. This should continue even after they have entered the world of work. This will ensure that they will be well equipped to take advantage of new opportunities that technological change will give rise to.

The Skill Development Fund (SDF) under the Ministry of Human Resources has already been established. It will assist those who are less fortunate to improve their economic prospects by making available loans for them to attend pre-employment skill training. Thus, not only are the training places and the career path established, the financial wherewithal is also in place.

For in-employment training, the Human Resources Development Fund (HRDF) has been the funding vehicle. More than 2.8 million training places involving financial assistance amounting to RM888.4 million have been funded. A proper fit between training and workplace requirements is in-built into the system with the training places nominated by the respective employers.

While the HRDF is employer-driven, the SDF will also extend funding facilities to those already at work to attend courses of their own choice. This is another component of the lifelong learning infrastructure.

The Ministry of Human Resources is about to embark on another strategic change in the area of skill training to better prepare Malaysians for the knowledge economy. Apart from the competency skills in the respective trades, the ITIs and ADTECs will introduce training in what is termed the 'critical enabling skills' among trainees. This refers to skills in effective communication, literacy and learning skills, creativity, problem solving, teamwork and leadership. These are generic skills that are relevant in all occupations to make our people lifelong learners. They are essential capabilities for knowledge workers. Apart from a revision to curriculum, this initiative will require a change in training method. Rather than mere exhortation of its virtues, there is need for experiential learning of these skills so they will be readily deployable once the trainees have entered the workplace. Lifelong learners are smarter people.

Cooperatives
Rising to New Demands and Challenges

Tan Sri Kasitah Gaddam
Minister, Ministry of Land and Co-operative Development

Rapid developments in technology, communications and world economies at the dawn of the new millennium have brought countries of the world closer together. The effects of globalisation have broken down barriers between countries and international markets and have a strong impact on local markets. Co-operatives, as well as other business operators today, must be able to respond to the rapidly changing world environment. Co-operatives need to be aware of the global context in which they operate and broaden their outlook to remain competitive.

The cooperative movement is based on universal values such as autonomy, self-help and mutual aid. It is essentially a socioeconomic movement with a moral responsibility and philosophy of its own. Co-operatives encourage people to realise their needs and achieve their aspirations by providing consumer goods, housing, health, insurance, transport, credits, employment, gender equality, protection for rural communities and enhanced standards of urban life.

In Malaysia, the cooperative movement has contributed substantially to the social and economic needs of its members. At the end of December 2000, there were 4,154 cooperative societies with a membership of over 4.4 million people, share capital of RM4.2 billion and assets of RM15.8 billion. Based on membership and its involvement in the various economic activities, the cooperative movement is gaining recognition as the third sector of the economy.

Rapid transformations in the role, structure and development of cooperatives have taken place. The new global environment demands practical exposure and the application of cooperative principles. Since the global market presents major challenges to the cooperative movement, cooperatives must make the necessary adjustments to remain competitive. It is recognised that the social dimension embedded in the cooperative philosophy is itself a valuable asset in the development of organisations, markets, human resources and outputs. The effects of globalisation on less prepared countries, the increasing uncontrolled movement of capital around the world, the increasing concentration of economic power in certain groups and the increasing number of people living in poverty show the expanding role and importance of cooperatives in the current world economies. To meet these challenges, cooperatives need to develop a vision towards building a new society where people, society and nature co-exist in harmony.

To be effective, cooperatives must have the capacity to harness professional management skills to realise values such as equality, mutuality, honesty, care, democracy and constructiveness. Managerial capacity must be recognised as part of the cooperative identity, central to the achievement of cooperative ideals and values in the 21st century. In other words, managerial development must combine cooperative values with commercial factors to succeed. Co-operatives must develop and empower their leaders, managers and members to realise their full potential.

Co-operatives are people-based organisations where the human factor is the overriding consideration. Co-operatives, undoubtedly, have the capacity to mobilise people in the movement to achieve a higher level of performance. The cooperative strength, which binds members together for their common good, can be a prime mover in economic development if harnessed productively.

Co-operatives too have business objectives. In an increasingly open and transparent environment, cooperatives must adhere to the practices of good governance in the management of their affairs. Good corporate governance will reduce the Government's involvement, which is in line with the people empowerment approach in any organisation.

Co-operatives are in the process of developing linkages and promoting amalgamation among themselves and with other suitable parties for mutual benefit. This will enable them to strategise and reposition themselves to compete effectively with others in the playing field. At the same time, members are expected to participate actively and respond positively to changing market conditions to ensure the success of their cooperatives. The 21st century offers opportunities for collaboration in education, health, research, information technology and other related fields.

The Government will continue to promote and assist the development of the cooperative movement in the country in line with Vision 2020. The Government has a responsibility to create an environment conducive for cooperatives to grow and succeed. In this respect, it is the intention of the Government to make the cooperative movement one of the movers or initiators of economic and social development in Malaysia. In line with this objective, the Government is advocating the principle, "let managers manage" in cooperatives to encourage initiative, talent, creativity and a result-oriented attitude.

The rapidly changing world environment today clearly reflects the need for cooperatives to strategise and reposition themselves to remain relevant. The cooperative movement has the capacity and the strength to leap forward to meet the challenges of today, tomorrow and the day after.

Primary Industries
Malaysia's Ingredients for Success

Dato' Seri Dr Lim Keng Yaik
Minister, Ministry of Primary Industries

One major success that Malaysia has achieved over the last century and which it can be proud of till today, is the development of the primary commodities sector. This sector has been instrumental in strengthening the country's economy, as we see it today, by providing the necessary foreign exchange earnings, income to the producers, employment opportunities as well as higher living standards for the rural populace. In 2000, the sector contributed 11.4% (RM42.69 billion, including commodity-based products) to total export earnings, 15.3% (RM31.103 billion, excluding commodity-based products) to the GDP and employed 14.9% (1.32 million) of the labour force. In fact, it has played a significant role in helping to cushion the economy from the impact of the recent economic problems. The success of the primary industries sector has been the product of many years of hard work, dedication and the commitment of various parties, aided by sound Government policies and political stability.

The ability to turn what seems to be virtually unknown commodities, not even indigenous to Malaysia as in the case of oil palm and rubber, into a wide variety of processed and manufactured products that are much sought after worldwide, is a major success story for the country. The rapid development of the sector was also due to the efforts of the Government which had the foresight in ensuring that the sector remains relevant while the country is being transformed to focus on the development of the secondary and tertiary sectors. In this context, the sector continues to evolve from merely producing and exporting primary raw materials to producing semi-processed and fully processed products, generating more value-added for the sector. Today, the primary commodities sector has made impressive progress in the area of downstream processing and turning out high value products that are in great demand by the world market. This augurs well for the country, contributing to its progress towards industrialised nation status in line with Vision 2020.

Looking back, it cannot be denied that although the country has been blessed with suitable land and agro-climatic conditions to develop the commodity sector, our success is largely attributed to the relentless efforts of the Government in formulating and implementing appropriate and effective policies and strategies, in cooperation with the private sector, to harness our God-given natural resources efficiently. The success of the primary industries sector has been due to the dynamic technological advancement in production, processing and end-use. Be it palm oil, rubber, timber, minerals or cocoa, this technology-led development has enabled the sector to continuously increase productivity, reduce costs of production, and widen its product base. Through the R&D activities, new and improved technologies are introduced which are also commercially-oriented. This is important as such efforts bring not only improved products to the marketplace, but also products capable of creating a niche in focused markets.

Malaysia is proud to be a leader in know-how and technology for a number of commodities such as palm oil, rubber, timber and minerals, particularly in the upstream plantation sector. These know-how and technology have been obtained through years of collaborative involvement in the industry by both the private sector and Government agencies, like the Malaysian Palm Oil Board (MPOB), the Malaysian Rubber Board (MRB), the Forest Research Institute of Malaysia (FRIM) and the Malaysian Cocoa Board (MCB). R&D has been an important instrument in protecting primary commodities against competing products. A classic example is the case of the smear campaign waged by the American Soyabean Association against palm oil, which we were able to counter with concerted nutrition research studies commissioned worldwide. These studies provided the scientific basis to confirm and reaffirm palm oil's positive qualities, particularly in terms of its nutritional values.

The success of the primary industries sector in Malaysia would not have materialised without the commitment and close cooperation between the Government and industry. Through regular and active consultations between the Government and various industry members on major matters of interest and common concern to the sector, the Government has been able to successfully formulate and implement sound policies which have proven effective in charting the healthy and sustainable growth of the sector. Furthermore, with financing contributed by the industry, the Government has been instrumental in ensuring that R&D and technical support serve the needs of the industry. These agencies have made important contributions in improving quality assurance, customer and market-oriented R&D and the promotion and marketing of the products of the sector.

These ingredients of success are still relevant today in ensuring that the sector continues to contribute significantly to the economy. As we move into the 21st century, we are facing more challenges. Even though presently we are still fortunate to have the wherewithal to keep us in the forefront of technology and development, as experienced by the palm oil, rubber, forestry and timber industries, new challenges are evolving. We have to also face emerging structural constraints and problems. We have to realise that the country no longer has an abundant supply of the traditional factors of production, in particular, land and labour. In order to push the industry further, we need to improve on the productive capacities of the sector by embarking on innovative technological advancement involving all levels of operations to significantly increase productivity, cut costs, improve quality, strengthen the market position and resolve labour constraints.

R&D is critical in ensuring a continued flow of innovative and high quality products to the market. The Government will continue to give greater emphasis to R&D to ensure that the primary industries sector continue to focus on increasing productivity as well as reducing cost of production, thus making our production units more efficient and our products more competitive in the marketplace. Apart from that, in addressing the issue of acute labour shortage in the country, particularly in the plantation sector, R&D in the area of labour-saving technologies or mechanisation is being given greater emphasis. Although some progress has been achieved in the palm oil and rubber sectors, a lot more effort has to be directed to ease the existing bottlenecks. Mechanisation is critical because the country must reduce its dependence on immigrant labour. The socioeconomic burden to the country may even outweigh the benefits we get from employing the foreign labour. Another area of focus for R&D is biotechnology which could open up new vistas and opportunities for the sector. Aside from producing better quality and higher yielding crop varieties, improved nutritional studies could be achieved. In this regard, research collaborations with local and reputable overseas universities and research institutions need to be further explored. The Government will continue to support the efforts of the private sector to be more involved in R&D.

The long-term viability of the primary industries sector depends on making a quantum leap in downstream value-added activities. While such a strategy is consistent with the thrust of the Second Industrial Master Plan, it is vital for improving producers' income as well as increasing foreign exchange earnings.

Opportunities are abundant in developing further downstream value addition. The palm oil industry is a case in point. The production of oleochemicals, especially final consumer products such as personal care products, detergents, pharmaceuticals and industrial products, provides immense potential. To further spearhead research into the use of palm-based oleochemicals, MPOB has set up the Advanced Oleochemicals Technology Centre. In addition, a new area which holds vast potential is the use of oil palm biomass. There is a huge amount of biomass available in the industry that can be converted into the production of high-value products such as medium density fibreboard, pulp and paper, furniture, animal feed and composite materials. Profiting from oil palm biomass is the way forward for the oil palm industry. In the case of rubber, the development of new rubber materials like epoxidised natural rubber, deproteinised natural rubber and thermoplastic natural rubber has opened up new applications especially in heavy-duty engineering, including the production of earthquake isolators. MRB has set up a modern Rubber Technology Centre to accelerate a programme for the industrialisation of rubber products. In the case of the cocoa industry, new uses for cocoa in the manufacturing of chocolate and cocoa confectionery and cocoa beverages are being expanded. For the timber industry, the manufacturing of high-end furniture, joinery and panel products as well as paper products and wood crafting are potentially beneficial investment opportunities.

The liberalisation of world trade will present both opportunities and threats to our primary products. Since Malaysia cannot isolate itself from the forces, we should take advantage of this by being more innovative as well as creative.

In order to make our presence felt and capture an increasing share of the overseas market, we not only have to move closer to the market segments, but we must also develop niches and establish loyal customers. This may involve establishing a chain of production processes in strategic locations around the world for primary products or by relocating manufacturing subprocesses such as palm oil refineries and bulking services overseas. At the same time, there is a need to synergise our strategies and programmes to changing consumer preferences, especially in matters associated with health and environmental concerns.

The success of the primary industries sector can also be attributed to the availability of a large pool of skilled and experienced manpower who have the expertise in managing various facets of the industries. Malaysia is in a position to extend its managerial expertise and experience to countries which are keen to develop their commodity sector through strategic alliances. In fact, some Malaysian companies have already ventured into neighbouring countries like Indonesia, Vietnam, the Philippines and Cambodia to develop joint-ventures in oil palm and timber. There are also good prospects in countries like Latin America, Africa and the South Pacific islands. The Ministry has always supported such offshore investment strategy, in line with the national policy of forging smart partnerships with countries of the South. Constrained by land and labour resources, Malaysia can no longer expand its plantation sector on its own. With all the experience accumulated over the years, Malaysia has both the technical capacity and capability as well as technology to make its presence useful overseas. This can be done by establishing joint-ventures as well as networking strategically with Third World countries on the basis of a win-win arrangement, so that Malaysians will continue to lead in the priority sectors by outsourcing its raw materials.

Recognising that globalisation and liberalisation are forces that Malaysia cannot avoid, Malaysia will continue to promote greater cooperation at the multilateral, regional and bilateral levels to resolve commodity issues, promote joint programmes and projects as well as to develop and expand trade in commodities. Malaysia will continue to be actively involved in negotiations with the World Trade Organisation to safeguard Malaysia's interests in the commodity sector. These include liberalising commodity trade and reducing subsidies, discriminatory and unilateral actions such as linking trade to non-trade related issues like environment and labour standards. At the regional level, Malaysia participates actively in various Asean fora and subregional arrangements in order to benefit further from greater cooperation in trade and investment.

In addition, bilateral issues affecting commodities will be taken up directly with the countries concerned. Through these bilateral talks and negotiations, we have succeeded in resolving some outstanding bilateral issues pertaining to market access, such as discriminatory tariff rates and quotas with specific countries. In view of recent developments in the rubber market, Malaysia signed an MOU with Thailand, the largest producer of rubber in the world, to establish joint efforts to improve the prices of rubber. Similar efforts are being extended to other major producers, such as Indonesia, in order to achieve a better impact for any joint strategy.

In line with the Government's commitment to conserve the environment and ecosystem, efforts will be directed towards strengthening sustainable forest management by adopting more environmentally-friendly production processes and technologies. Besides that, in an effort to perpetuate the role of forests as a source of timber and non-timber products and other intangible benefits, the area under the Permanent Reserve Forest will be maintained and managed on a sustainable basis. The establishment of forest plantations will be given greater emphasis to augment domestic timber supply in the future. Under this programme, suitable tree species will be planted, including rubber plantations, to meet the increasing demand of the timber-based industries.

Realising the important role of the mineral sector in the national economy, the Government formulated the National Mineral Policy aimed at providing the foundation for the development of an effective, efficient and competitive regulatory environment that will allow the mineral sector to expand, diversify and contribute to the country's economic development. Although metallic minerals such as tin, copper and gold have declined in terms of their contribution to the export earnings, the major thrust of the mineral industry in the future will be in the industrial mineral sector, where possibilities are expected to be enormous.

From a macro point of view, the primary industries sector has a high degree of linkage with the economy because of the high local content of the output produced. Development of the sector could help to retain the wealth that it generates within the country. Studies point to vast possibilities in terms of value-added as appropriate technologies are available. Recognising that the sector needs to be modernised through the injection of new technologies for material conversion and mining, efforts will be directed towards opening up the sector to foreign players. This will ensure the adoption of more environmentally-friendly processes in mineral exploration and expansion.

The Oil & Gas Industry
Providing Energy for the Future

Petroliam Nasional Bhd

The petroleum industry in Malaysia has undergone tremendous transformation especially during the last two and a half decades following the establishment of Petroliam Nasional Bhd (Petronas) as the national oil company on August 17, 1974, and the enactment of the Petroleum Development Act in October of the same year. Vested with the exclusive ownership and control of the entire petroleum resources in the country under the Act, Petronas has in effect become the sole concessionaire with the right and responsibility to develop the nation's petroleum resources.

In the early years, Petronas' focus was on developing these resources by promoting oil and gas exploration, development and production activities in the country through production sharing contracts (PSCs) with various multinational petroleum corporations. While developing the upstream sector, Petronas has also actively expanded and diversified into various downstream ventures to realise its mission of developing and adding value to the country's petroleum resources to ensure that the people as a whole enjoy the full benefits from the development of Malaysia's petroleum industry.

Since then, Malaysia's oil and gas industry has been charting consistent and continuous growth in both the upstream and downstream sectors. The development of the industry has contributed significantly to the overall economic growth of the country, not only in meeting energy needs, but also in terms of investment, foreign exchange earnings, human resources development, technology transfer and new business and employment opportunities.

Moving forward in this new millennium, the country's oil and gas sector will indeed play an increasingly important role in supporting the continuing development of the Malaysian economy towards realising its Vision 2020. The energy sector in Malaysia, like in any other country, is the backbone of the economy. For Malaysia to achieve its socioeconomic development objectives, it is vital to ensure an adequate and secure supply of energy in the country. To this end, Malaysia's long-term energy policies and strategies for the future will need to focus on the issue of depleting oil resources and greater efforts in reducing the country's dependence on oil. Efforts to achieve the objectives of the National Energy Diversification Policy of 1979 are therefore expected to be intensified with increasing emphasis on the development of gas as a clean and environmentally-friendly alternative fuel. There will also be a new focus on developing renewable energy fuels in the future.

With the abundant gas reserves which are four times larger than the oil reserves in the country and its established gas infrastructure already in place, Petronas is well-poised to propel Malaysia forward in the gas industry, particularly at the regional level. Its completed Peninsular Gas Utilisation (PGU) pipeline system will provide a strong foundation for the future development of a Trans-Asean Gas Pipeline (TAGP) system, identified as one of the six energy cooperation programmes to establish the Trans-Asean Energy Network within the Asean Vision 2020 framework adopted by the

Second Asean Informal Summit held in Kuala Lumpur in 1997. The realisation of the TAGP project will ensure a more secure and stable supply of energy for Malaysia and the region in the future.

The PGU pipeline system which was started in 1984 and developed by Petronas in three phases involved the construction of 2,000 km of gas transmission pipelines and six gas processing plants with a total capacity of 2,000 million standard cubic feet per day (mmscfd) of gas. The PGU system will be linked to the Trans-Thailand-Malaysia Gas Pipeline System through the take-off point at Changlun, Kedah and connected to the Malaysia-Thailand Joint Development Area (JDA) via Songkhla, Southern Thailand, to enable the transportation of gas from the JDA fields through the PGU system.

This project represents one of the various initiatives undertaken by Petronas to help spearhead the development of Malaysia's gas resources. The project has provided Petronas' production-sharing contractors with the opportunity to develop and monetise the gas reserves previously discovered but not utilised. This in turn has provided the nation with a cleaner and more environmentally-friendly alternative fuel for power generation required for its industrialisation process. Today, gas makes up more than 70% of the energy mix for power generation in Malaysia.

The PGU project has also spawned the development of the petrochemical industry in the country by providing the gas feedstock required by the industry for the manufacture of a myriad of petrochemical products for both the domestic and export markets. To ensure a well-planned and systematic development of the petrochemical industry, Petronas is developing two integrated petrochemical complexes (IPCs) in the Eastern Corridor of Peninsular Malaysia, namely the ethylene-based IPC in Kertih, Terengganu and the propylene-based IPC in Gebeng, Pahang. The integration of petrochemical plants with related operations supported by common infrastructural facilities like the Central Utilities and Storage Facilities housed within the IPC is aimed at optimising synergistic advantages while enhancing cost effectiveness and efficiency. The IPCs will help realise Petronas' aspiration to turn Malaysia into a regional petrochemical hub.

Petronas has taken a step further in promoting the use of natural gas with the introduction of the gas district cooling (GDC) and co-generation system, which is essentially a centralised energy plant generating chilled water for air-conditioning and the production of electricity and other necessary utilities for buildings. The GDC and Co-generation System, which uses natural gas as its main fuel, has been successfully installed in the Kuala Lumpur City Centre where the Petronas Twin Towers are located, the Kuala Lumpur International Airport and Putrajaya, the Federal Government's Administrative Centre.

To promote the use of gas in the transportation sector, Petronas launched the Natural Gas for Vehicles (NGV) programme in the Klang Valley in 1991 with the completion of the second phase of the PGU project. Various incentives are provided to encourage the motoring public to use NGV while ongoing efforts are being undertaken to expand the NGV refuelling facilities in the country as well as to enhance public awareness on NGV and its benefits.

In line with its strategy to optimise the use of the country's natural gas resources and to help reduce air pollution, Petronas launched its prototype Enviro 2000 NGV taxi in 1996. Powered by a four-cylinder 2000 cc NGV monogas engine, the Enviro 2000 taxis began commercial operation during the 1998 Commonwealth Games in Kuala Lumpur. Today, there are a thousand Enviro 2000 taxis in Kuala Lumpur, symbolising a national initiative to ensure the provision of public transport that is environmentally-friendly, efficient and economical.

While gas will assume an increasingly important role in meeting future energy needs, the years ahead will see further energy diversification efforts being explored in the form of developing renewable energy sources such as wind, solar and biomass (e.g. palm oil and wood wastes) towards enhancing the reliability and security of energy supply in Malaysia.

In this respect, Petronas, jointly with the Palm Oil Research Institute of Malaysia (PORIM), is looking into the possibility of developing palm oil diesel as an alternative cleaner, renewable fuel. Petronas is also sponsoring a local university's R&D project on solar energy.

Against this backdrop, the years ahead promise to be both exciting and challenging. Petronas, in leading the further development of the oil and gas industry in Malaysia, will continue to play an important role in helping to ensure and enhance the security of energy supply to fuel the future success of Malaysia in its journey towards realising its vision of becoming a fully developed nation by the year 2020.

Infrastructure

Property

Housing the Nation—Strategies and Programmes

Dato' Seri Ong Ka Ting
Minister, Ministry of Housing and Local Government

An important social goal of national development is the provision of housing to the population. In Malaysia's socioeconomic development plans, it has been the Government's overriding priority to provide adequate, decent and affordable shelter for its population, particularly the lower income groups. It has been recognised that, apart from fulfilling basic needs, the housing industry also contributes towards the economic growth of the nation.

HOUSING POLICY AND STRATEGIES

The main objective of Malaysia's housing policy is to ensure that all Malaysians, especially the lower income groups, have access to decent, affordable and adequate housing. To achieve this objective, several housing development strategies have been adopted for implementation through the five-year development plans and the long-term development plans. These major housing strategies are:

i. Emphasising and encouraging the construction of more low-cost and low-medium-cost houses, especially in the urban areas, to reflect more realistically the housing requirements of the majority of the people.
ii. Encouraging the provision of more houses for rental to overcome the immediate need for shelter, especially for lower income families in major urban centres and to alleviate the problem of urban squatters. Rental of low-cost housing would also include, where possible, the option on the part of eligible tenants to eventually purchase such units.
iii. Greater emphasis on the human settlement concept in the planning and development of housing projects. Housing development will be viewed in the broader context of creating a decent and viable human settlement. Housing project developers are required to provide adequate basic infrastructure while the relevant authorities will provide other social amenities like schools, clinics, community halls, sports/recreational and other facilities necessary for a better quality of life.
iv. Greater participation by the private sector, particularly in the provision of low and low-medium-cost housing.

FUTURE SCENARIOS

The development of the cybercities (Putrajaya and Cyberjaya) and the Multimedia Super Corridor (MSC) provides ample opportunities for the construction of new houses in Malaysia during the Eighth Malaysia Plan period. Besides Putrajaya and Cyberjaya, 12 other new urban centres will be developed. These growth areas include Georgetown-Butterworth and its conurbation, the Johor Baru-Pasir Gudang Industrial Zone, the Ipoh-Lumut corridor and Melaka-Air Keroh in the western belt as well as Temerloh-Mentakab and Kuantan-Kota Baru in the eastern corridor.

With the country's economy growing at an average rate of 7% per annum over the last decade, the income per capita has increased from RM6,298 in 1990 to RM12,863 in 2000 and is projected to reach RM25,000 in the year 2020. Simultaneously, the poverty rate has also declined from 17.1% to 6% and is expected to decline to 1.2% over the same period. With rising income and reduced poverty conditions, a substantial proportion of the Malaysian society will become more affluent and will be able to acquire quality houses with improved physical and social facilities.

Malaysia's population is projected to touch 23.3 million by the end of 2000 and 25 million by the year 2005. Whilst the national population has increased in number, the household size has declined considerably. The average household size is expected to shrink to 3.6 persons by the first quarter of this century with greater reductions taking place in the urban areas. By the year 2020, the country's population is expected to breach the 32 million mark with about 75% being urban dwellers.

A larger population, an increasing number of nuclear families, loss of housing stock (resulting from units demolished for development, infrastructure upgrading, resettling squatters, etc.) and rapid industrialisation imply greater housing requirements.

HOUSING PROGRAMMES

In Malaysia, the fulfilment of housing needs has been identified under successive five-year plans as a major social objective. Housing programmes are formulated based on housing needs and take into consideration population trends, growth rates, household size, family structure, household income distribution, affordability, housing type preferences, conditions of existing housing stock, construction capacity, availability of resources, bridging and end-financing and the extent of squatter settlements.

Under the Seventh Malaysia Plan, 1996-2000, a total of 800,000 units of houses are needed to meet the increasing number of new families and replacements. The breakdown of the housing targets and projected performance by types of houses is shown in Table 1. To ensure that the provision of housing will be fairly distributed, about 550,000 units (70%) will be low and low-medium cost units.

For the Eighth Malaysia Plan, 2001-2005, the Government will continue to ensure that all Malaysians, particularly the lower income groups, have access to adequate and affordable homes and related facilities. About 615,000 units are envisaged as an achievable target to be built during the Plan period. A reorientation of some past policy strategies and new measures will be incorporated to effectively fulfil the housing needs of the growing population and,at the same time, further develop the domestic housing industry. Towards this end, the Ministry of Housing and Local Government has proposed various housing programmes:

- Public Low-Cost Housing Programmes (continuation and new) for sale and rental.
- Maintenance Programme for Public Low-Cost Houses.
- Formulation of an integrated National Housing Policy.
- Establishment of the Malaysian Human Settlement and Urbanisation Research Institute (MAHSURI) for research and development activities and as a depository of information on human settlement and urbanisation.
- Implementation of the Modular Co-ordination Concept to improve the quality of housing and reduce costs in the production of mass housing.
- Introduction of the open Industrialised Building System in the housing industry.

Sector	7th Plan Target	1996	1997	1998	1999	2000	1996 –2000	% Achieved
PUBLIC AND PRIVATE	800,000	106,701	132,562	162,631	160,000	140,000	701,894	87.7
Low-Cost	235,000	26,683	33,355	41,537	39,141	34,249	174,965	74.5
Low-Medium-Cost	350,000	11,445	14,715	18,123	14,629	12,801	71,713	20.5
Medium & High-Cost	215,000	68,573	84,492	102,971	106,230	92,950	455,216	211.7
PUBLIC	230,000	17,707	26,860	37,792	32,500	28,437	143,296	62.3
Low-Cost	95,000	9,065	12,429	16,823	14,916	13,052	66,285	69.8
Low-Medium-Cost	110,000	2,115	3,632	5,034	4,190	3,666	18,636	16.9
Medium & High-Cost	25,000	6,528	10,799	15,935	13,394	11,719	58,375	233.5
PRIVATE	570,000	88,994	105,702	124,839	127,500	111,563	558,598	98.0
Low-Cost	140,000	17,618	20,926	24,714	24,225	21,197	108,680	77.6
Low-Medium-Cost	240,000	9,331	11,083	13,089	10,439	9,135	53,077	22.1
Medium & High-Cost	190,000	62,045	73,693	87,036	92,836	81,231	396,841	208.9

Source: Ministry of Housing and Local Government, National Housing Department, October 2000

FUTURE HOUSING DIRECTIONS

As the nation progresses through the new millennium, an appropriate vision is that of housing the nation within a balanced living environment equipped with urban facilities, social and recreational amenities, and conducive and sustainable economic opportunities. To achieve these objectives, specific strategies encompassing economic, human resource, technological and environmental aspects need to be considered.

Among the economic and cross-sectoral aspects are determining an adequate supply of affordable houses and the preparation of a National Spatial Plan to eradicate the disparities and imbalances that exist among ethnic groups, regions and sectors.

The emerging trend in the housing industry is the use of innovative construction technology. Future technology will depend more on the electronic and telecommunication multimedia systems than on the physical materials that developers currently use for the industry. The MSC holds the greatest promise for electronically wired and connected future homes that will, within the next several years, significantly affect housing design and internal space use and layout. This will enable the creation of the "smart' house with interactive functions for business, retail, government-related transactions, recreation and education which were virtually unheard of years ago.

A further aspect of future housing design that is gaining greater attention is the impact of housing development on the natural environment. There has to be responsible concern in the housing industry for a sustainable future arising from the clearing of land for housing construction, the use of materials and energy resources and the enormous amount of waste emitted from these developments. Greater efforts have been accorded to managing waste discharge (solid, household and liquid) in terms of recycling or returning to the environment with minimal environmental impact. Therefore, future housing development should pay greater attention to the plan layouts and build configurations along passive low-energy designs.

Conclusion

The Government will concentrate more on meeting the social objective of providing sufficient and decent houses at affordable prices to meet the growing needs of the masses, particularly the lower income groups. A timely review of housing policy and regulations, strategies and action plans is essential to achieve housing goals in this millennium.

Transport

Moving Rapidly into the Future

Dato' Seri Dr Ling Liong Sik
Minister, Ministry of Transport

Nurturing the intertwined areas of transport and logistics is crucial to the economic wellbeing of Malaysia. In the absence of a healthy transport and logistics system, goods cannot be efficiently to markets and Malaysia would certainly not be such an open, export-oriented economy. A well-developed and integrated transport and logistics network is thus vital for economic growth. With the increasing trend towards globalisation, it is even more imperative that the Malaysian transport and logistics sector enhances its competitiveness to meet the challenges of the global market.

As Malaysia moves into the new millennium, development of the transport sector will be further intensified. Already, a considerable amount has been expended to ensure that Malaysia has the necessary infrastructure and capacity to support continued growth. Under the Seventh Malaysia Plan (1996 to 2000), the public sector has incurred more than RM20.5 billion for the development of the transport sector. Of this, RM12.3 billion has been spent for roads, RM1.3 billion for airports and RM1.1 million for ports. For rail and urban transport, RM5.4 billion and RM0.4 billion have been spent respectively. From 1996 to 2000, private sector investment in privatised transport projects totalled more than RM38 billion.

Growth Spurt

The demand for transport and logistic services in a country is normally a function of its economic growth. Industrialisation and international trade are two key factors that have jointly transformed the Malaysian economy and fuelled an increasing demand for transport and logistics services.

Over the last four decades, the Malaysian economy has evolved significantly. In the 1950s and 1960s, Malaysia was primarily an agro-based economy dominated by rubber, palm oil, pepper and timber. However, the country pursued a policy of economic diversification in the 1960s by concentrating not only on primary goods but also manufactured products. Since manufacturing was in its infancy, import substitution was a key strategy to economic restructuring. This import substitution phase was succeeded by a decade of export orientation in the 1970s.

In the 1980s, a focused regimen combining an emphasis on exports and a marked bias towards the electronics and hi-tech industries further promoted Malaysia's transformation into a manufacturing-based economy. In 1986, the government launched the First Industrial Master Plan, which focused on further expanding and upgrading export-oriented resource-based and non resource-based industries such as the electronics and electrical goods industries.

The 1990s saw another advancement in the evolution of Malaysia's manufacturing sector. The emphasis switched to high technology, capital intensive and value-added industries. Manufacturing continued to register rapid growth, accounting for 30% of Gross Domestic Product (GDP) by 1999 compared to 14.8% in 1970.

THE GROWTH OF TRANSPORT

As the economic pace picked up, transport had to keep pace with the rapid growth of manufacturing and industrialisation. In line with this, the transport sector's share of the GDP increased from 6.8% in 1990 to 8.0% in 2000. Over the years, the thrust of transport sector development has been to increase capacity and improve efficiency.

ROADS

Road development was based on a three-pronged strategy, which was to increase the road network, alleviate capacity constraints and expand the road network to open up new growth centres.

Malaysia's road network increased by 19.2% from 53,984 kilometres in 1990 to 64,328 kilometres in 1995. Public sector expenditure of RM1.8 billion and private sector funding of RM17.5 billion financed the construction of the additional roads. During this period, the East-West Highway was completed and the 847-kilometre North-South Expressway was opened, linking Johor Baru in the south with Bukit Kayu Hitam in the north, bordering Thailand. The North-South Expressway reduced travel time by half and curtailed vehicle owners' travelling and operational costs considerably.

The road network subsequently expanded to 66,774 kilometres in 1999. From 1995 to 2000, an additional 16,100 kilometres of roads, modern highways and urban road systems have been built, with investments of RM12.3 billion and RM16 billion by the public and private sectors respectively.

RAIL

Rail development was aimed at increasing capacity and enhancing operational safety for both freight and passenger services, both locally and regionally.

By 1995, Malaysia's railway tracks measured 2,227 kilometres. From 1996 to 2000, rail development focused extensively on double tracking and electrification, and included two massive light rail transit projects to ease urban transport woes.

Cargo transit centres were also developed further. Notably, the container yard in Padang Besar was expanded, which improved operational efficiency and increased the volume of container haulage between Thailand and Peninsular Malaysia.

Efforts to expand and modernise the rail system nationwide have cost the public and private sectors almost RM11 billion over the past five years.

Ports

Port development has also focused on expanding capacity, upgrading and increasing equipment and facilities in order to improve the efficiency of ports and related operations. Thanks to concerted efforts by the public and private sector, the nation's maritime ports have enjoyed capacity expansion and access to improved equipment and facilities.

Total port capacity increased from 174.1 million tonnes in 1995 to 344 million tonnes in 2000. Likewise, the volume of cargo handled increased from 152.3 million tonnes in 1995 to 220.8 million tonnes in 2000.

Public sector expenditure for ports was more than RM1.1 million from 1996 to 2000. Operators of privatised ports invested more than RM4 billion in expanding capacity and constructing new port facilities.

Airports

Similarly, airport development has been geared towards growing capacity and upgrading facilities in order to fulfil rising demand for air travel and freight services. Based on 9% growth per annum for air cargo, Malaysian airports handled more than 773,000 tonnes of cargo in 2000. During 1996 to 2000, more than RM9 billion was expended in the construction of the Kuala Lumpur International Airport (KLIA) at Sepang. The Government intends to develop KLIA into a regional hub for both passengers and cargo.

Transport and Logistics Services

Concurrently, related transport and logistics services or cargo handling also enjoyed healthy demand, thanks to the buoyant economy. GDP is expected to more than double during the period of the Second Industrial Master Plan (1996-2005) from RM120 billion in 1995 to RM256 billion in 2005. Manufacturing contributed RM39 billion or more than 30% to total GDP in 1999 against expectations of 38.4% or RM98 billion in 2005. There will be even greater demand for transport and logistics services in order to move these goods to markets.

All along, there has been a strong correlation between industrialisation and demand for transport and logistics services. As Malaysia industrialised, such demand skyrocketed, as evidenced by the number of transport vehicles plying along the arteries of the Malaysian transport system.

Land transportation comprises the movement of general and loose cargo by conventional lorries or trucks, containerised cargo by prime movers and mixed cargo by rail.

The number of registered goods vehicles used for domestic goods transport increased from 420,000 in 1995 to 642,976 in 1999, equivalent to an impressive growth rate of 25% per annum. According to a 1996 study, more than 70% of domestic cargo is transported by road.

Container haulage also progressed significantly. In 1980, total containers handled were 123,000 TEUs (20-ft equivalent units), rising to more than 900,000 TEUs in 1990 and surpassing 3.7 million

TEUs in 1999. Again, industrialisation and international trade accounted for the upsurge in container throughput. Assuming 10% growth per annum from 2000 to 2010, the present volume is likely to more than triple, exceeding 10 million TEUs. Currently, the regulated container haulage industry has 20 players. They operate more than 3,000 prime movers and 15,000 trailers in Peninsular Malaysia alone.

Seaborne cargo, whether containerised, general, liquid or dry, also faces a bright future. By 2010, seaborne cargo is projected to increase to more than 660 million tonnes compared to 200 million tonnes now. With efforts to transform Port Klang into a national load centre and transshipment hub, total cargo volume could increase by another 40%.

By 2010, the total tonnage to be handled by local ports could exceed one billion tonnes.

Airborne cargo also grew significantly from about 241,000 tonnes in 1990 to about 482,000 tonnes in 1995 and more than 770,000 tonnes in 2000. As Malaysia upgrades its industrial base with the manufacture of high-end and value-added electronic products for the export markets, air cargo volume can be expected to increase significantly. By 2010, air cargo volume should surpass 1.6 million tonnes, assuming a 10% growth rate per annum from 2001 to 2010.

Although growth was slower in rail freight cargo, this sector also demonstrated a reasonable increase of 13% from 1990's 4.6 million tonnes to 1995's 5.2 million tonnes. In terms of container traffic, volume grew by 45% from 94,403 TEUs in 1990 to 137,000 TEUs in 1995. Based on a 10% growth per annum, the volume of containerised cargo by rail could hit 380,000 TEUs by 2010. Total freight traffic could exceed 17 million tonnes by 2010.

FUTURE DEVELOPMENT AND TRENDS

The anticipated growth in cargo volumes augurs well for the transport and logistics operators. By 2010, the volume of cargo can be expected to increase at least three-fold, assuming a consistent growth rate of 10% per annum from 2001 to 2010. But this is a conservative forecast. During the 1990 to 1997 economic boom, Malaysian cargo volumes rose at an explosive rate of between 15% and 20%.

The need for immense infrastructure developments in the transport and logistics sector presents great business opportunities for both governments and corporations to build cross-border links. Currently, Asean authorities are studying the feasibility of establishing the Trans-Asian Railway Project connecting Peninsular Malaysia to Kunming in Southern China via Thailand, Laos, Cambodia and Vietnam. In addition, the Malaysian transport authorities are actively involved in the East Coast Highway project, connecting the West Coast states of Peninsular Malaysia with the oil and gas corridor in Terengganu on the East Coast.

However, these new developments and investments are not just a boost for the transport and logistics industry, which is one of the eight industry clusters earmarked for development under Malaysia's Second Industrial Master Plan. For instance, opportunities relating to equipment, manufacture and sales of trucks, prime movers and forklifts will abound. The equipment manufacturing industry will in turn need support from the component and spare parts industry. Business opportunities in this area alone should be worth several billion ringgit.

Since transport providers will be concentrating on their core businesses, engineering support services such as repair and maintenance jobs will likely be outsourced. This will promote the growth of engineering support service industries since more than 50% of operating costs are related to engineering needs, such as repair, maintenance, spare parts, tyres and tubes. New depots, warehouses and distribution parks are expected to mushroom to meet growing cargo handling requirements, providing construction opportunities.

Technological change will also shape the face of the transport and logistics sector. Companies indifferent to technology will find it an uphill task to compete globally. Transport and logistics providers must be able to offer value-added services enhanced by the Internet and new technologies. Companies should be utilising the Net to provide customers with e-commerce services, such as tracking and tracing information, document preparation and automated customs clearance. E-commerce will facilitate round-the-clock, real-time operations.

Malaysia offers tremendous opportunities for e-commerce development in the transport and logistics sector. Other investment spin-offs revolve around the local manufacture of global tracking equipment for cargo and related software. In tune with current trends, transport operators will be investing substantially in Information Technology, in order to reinvent the way they do business.

In the new millennium, transport and logistics providers must adapt themselves to the supply or value chain between manufacturers and consumers. The role of these operators is no longer confined to providing common services to all and sundry. Instead, they have to undertake a dedicated or specialised role in a particular value chain, providing entire distribution, warehousing and logistics services.

Last but not least, developing the muscle of the local transport and logistics sector will help reduce the country's balance of payments. According to Bank Negara Malaysia, freight and insurance accounted for a deficit of RM9.7 billion in 1999.

To make Malaysia more self-sufficient in terms of freight and shipping, the Government is committed to developing a world-class transport and logistics system that will serve Malaysia well in the global marketplace.

Works Ministry
Maintaining Roads, Buildings and Water Supply

Dato' Seri S. Samy Vellu
Minister, Ministry of Works

Good infrastructure and reliable basic amenities are essential elements in the smooth running of a nation.

In Malaysia, the Ministry of Works holds the crucial task of ensuring that these elements are upgraded and maintained in order to cater to economic and societal demands. Under the country's development blueprint, the Eighth Malaysia Plan, Malaysian infrastructure must grow at a pace that can accommodate the twin requirements of rising economic growth and a burgeoning and increasingly sophisticated population.

ROADS

Under the auspices of the Ministry of Works, the road network in Malaysia has been expanding, thanks to investment by both the public and private sector. In addition to existing roads and highways such as the Federal Highway, new roads such as the billion-ringgit North-South Expressway (NSE) and the Lebuhraya Damansara-Puchong (LDP) have sprouted in recent years to accommodate increased transportation demands.

Malaysian roads consist of both public and privatised road networks. Federal Roads, which are separate from privatised roads such as the North-South Expressway, are funded directly by the Federal Government. The funds are allocated to the Federal Public Works Department (PWD) for administrative and maintenance purposes. Although states are responsible for maintaining their own roads via their own PWDs, the Federal Government also funds the maintenance of State Roads via an annual State Road Grant.

As part of road maintenance, the PWD relies on sophisticated computer systems for pavement management, bridge management, and slope maintenance and inspection. Some of these systems have even been developed in-house, demonstrating PWD creativity.

For instance, the Pavement Appraisal and Management Suite (PAMS) is used by the PWD to present cases and to raise issues on road maintenance budgets to policy makers. In addition, PWD uses PAMS to establish the optimum maintenance strategy for pavements and to obtain maximum value from pavement investments.

The PWD also uses a Bridge Management System called JKR BMS, developed in-house by the Bridge Unit of Roads Branch PWD. Designed to accommodate the specific needs of PWD, the BMS consists of seven modules, which include the following: Data entry enables the entry and storage of bridge data such as bridge condition and history data; Bridge Information allows the retrieval of information on a specific bridge or group of bridges; and Bridge Priority allocates priority ranking among all bridges or groups of bridges for improvement and maintenance work in a systematic manner. This system has enabled a more systematic management of bridges.

PWD also uses a slope priority ranking system (which was developed in-house) to prioritise slope maintenance and rehabilitation works. With such prioritisation, it is hoped that the risks of slope failures to road users are minimised.

The PWD also works to ensure that road development has a minimal impact on the environment. Under the Environmental Quality (Prescribed Activities) (Environmental Impact Assessment) Order 1987, Environmental Impact Assessments must be carried out before the construction of expressways and national highways are begun, in order to assess the impact of road-building on the environment. The PWD has produced a set of guidelines entitled "The Environmental Impact Assessment of Highway/Road Projects", completed in 1993 with technical and financial assistance from the World Bank.

These guidelines state that the purpose of carrying out an EIA test is to assess the potential negative impact on the environment due to the construction of a road project.

EIA tests also seek to avoid costly mistakes in project implementation, either because of the environmental damage likely to arise during project implementation, or because of modifications that may be required subsequently in order to make the project environmentally acceptable.

Road safety is also an important facet of the road authorities' duties. In order to reduce the number of accident rates by 30% in 2000 compared to the base year of 1989, road authorities are practising Accident Prevention and Accident Reduction.

Under Accident Prevention, Road Safety Auditing has been carried out for all existing and new roads during the planning, design, construction and operation stages of a project. Road Safety audits can identify potential safety problems.

Accident Reduction, on the other hand, will attempt to mitigate the danger of hazardous locations along existing roads. The latter also entails carrying out research and study programmes to identify hazardous or blackspot locations. Road surfaces, geometric standards and traffic control devices are also studied to determine their efficacy in improving road safety.

Under Phase One of the Road Safety Programme, the Highway Planning Unit of the Ministry of Works identified over 100 accident-prone areas along the major and minor Federal roads in the country. Then, with financial aid from the World Bank, the PWD improved the conditions at 42 of these locations and constructed 27 pedestrian bridges at a total cost of RM86 million.

Construction

Construction is a core activity of the Ministry of Works, the agency responsible for the implementation of government buildings and infrastructures like bridges and dams. The Ministry, through its implementation arm, PWD, has significantly contributed towards building the nation and the continuous development of the building and construction industry. As Malaysia aspires to be a developed nation, the need for a comprehensive policy towards industrial development in the building sector becomes crucial.

Recognising its role as a major player in the nation's construction industry, the Ministry, together with the PWD, are actively pursuing a programme for change to promote open industrialisation in the building industry via the 'Malaysia Incorporated' concept which encourages cooperation and interaction between the public and private sectors.

Open industrialisation is a long-term and systematic approach towards an overhaul of the building industry. An organised process, industrialisation calls for the active participation of all relevant parties in the public and private sectors. The open system is a method of organising the building industry on a national and international level, taking advantage of an open market for building components that fit together, geometrically and functionally, for a wide variety of building types. It requires detailed organisation of building activities such as the production, transportation and erection of the various building components at the worksite to achieve a shorter construction period and efficient management of resources and investments.

Open industrialisation promotes standardisation, which in turn facilitates prefabrication, thus encouraging the growth of a components industry. Industrial production or prefabrication of modular building components offers a wide selection of multi-usable building components that are compatible and easily assembled in different designs. This will enhance efficiency in the building industry by significantly reducing construction time due to the reduced amount of cast-in-situ work and speedy building assembly, lowering manpower requirement due to extensive mechanisation, increasing quality control and substantially reducing wastage and lowering overall construction cost.

Given the rapid growth in the building industry, it is imperative that the industry is committed towards continuous upgrading to maintain a competitive edge in the local and global market.

Water Supply

Efficiency, conservation and growth are also watchwords in the water supply sector. The nation's water resources and infrastructure need to be managed properly and holistically in order to ensure adequate supplies of clean water for Malaysia's growing population and industries.

The proposed National Water Policy and the new National Water Resources Master Plan (covering the planning horizon up to 2050) will provide the strategic plans and guiding principles for the future development and conservation of the country's water resources. These principles are based on integrated development, the equitable regional allocation of water resources, environmental integrity, uniform water regulation and practices, the economic value of water and uniform water tariff structure. This will be complemented by the use of regulatory mechanisms to enforce compliance to meet environmental and water quality objectives.

Besides implementing a safe, efficient and reliable service, there are also concerns with water wastage and water losses. All states face two major problems with regard to water supply: growing demand due to an increasing population, particularly in urban centres and an ageing pipe network which is no longer able to be maintained or expanded to efficiently deliver water.

An effective and comprehensive demand management and conservation strategy, an integral part of the sustainable water policy, has been put in place to solve this problem. Under this approach, water demand management will not only augment, but more importantly, "stretch" existing supplies and delay the development of large capital-intensive structures until ample analysis has been carried out. A crucial part of water demand management is tackling leakages. Water losses and water unaccounted for will be reduced from 36% in 2000 to 31% in 2005 via a plan to replace existing asbestos cement pipelines and refurbish old treatment plants.

To support demand management and conservation, more efforts will be directed towards raising awareness and public education to stress the critical importance of water in daily life and the need for conservation even in non-crisis times.

The national water supply coverage is now 92%, with almost 100% coverage for urban areas and 87% for rural areas. In addition to providing for increasing urban demands, the government will continue to emphasise the importance of providing additional good quality drinking water to small rural communities to improve quality of life and facilitate economic growth. With these new additions, national rural water supply coverage should increase from 87% in 1999 to 91% in 2005. Rural coverage will improve to 95% for

Kedah, Pahang, Perlis, Terengganu and Sarawak and 60% for Kelantan and Sabah.

The implementation of water supply projects is being accelerated with the construction of the Chereh Dam, the Greater Kuantan Water Supply scheme and the Tanjung Malim Water Supply scheme. These schemes will contribute to the growth of the industrial areas located in the vicinity of the two townships. Construction of the Sungai Selangor Phase 3 Project (SSP3) and the Pahang-Selangor Raw Water Transfer scheme is being undertaken to cater for the continued increase in water demand and to solve the current water shortage in the Klang Valley. The SSP3 consists of the Sungai Selangor Dam, and Stages 1 and 2 of the Water Treatment Plant at Sungai Badong. Stage 1 will be completed by 2002 and Stage 2 by 2004. The first giant raw water transfer project from Pahang to Selangor is scheduled for completion by 2006. This project is expected to transfer an ultimate capacity of 2400 MLD of raw water by means of pipelines and a tunnel from Pahang to Selangor, the Federal Territory of Kuala Lumpur and at a much later date, to Negeri Sembilan. The project is also aimed at meeting projected demands to ensure uninterrupted future water supplies for domestic and industrial needs in the three regions since a critical shortfall of available water resources in Selangor is expected to occur by 2006.

Current and projected population growth is expanding the demand for water, for drinking, sanitation, commercial and industrial uses, and recreational and aesthetic purposes. Demand for domestic and industrial use is expected to increase by 5.4% per annum between 2001 and 2005.

In addition to implementing new projects to expand capacity, steps will be taken to manage demand through conservation measures, reduction of pipe leakages, new sources of supply and protection, and conservation of water catchments and watershed areas. Given the experience of the 1998 water crisis in the Klang

Valley, efforts will be taken to improve monitoring and surveillance as a water management technique which will also act as an early warning system. Such measures include close monitoring of dam characteristics such as hydrological yield, storage volume, critical level and mode of release of water for better balancing of supply and demand, particularly during the dry season. The construction of more storage bunds will also be considered. The feasibility and commercial viability of the use of ground water as a source will be further explored while detailed contingency plans will be drawn up to enable proper response to occurrences of water crisis.

Johore, Kelantan, Penang and Terengganu have already privatised or corporatised their state water supply services while Selangor and Negeri Sembilan are expected to complete the privatisation process sometime during the initial period of the Eighth Malaysia Plan. Sabah, Pahang, Perak and Malacca are expected to complete their schemes during the Eighth Malaysia Plan. In line with privatisation guidelines, privatisation of water supply will be conducted in a holistic approach, including source works, treatment works, distribution of water, billing and customer service. State regulatory bodies are set up with sufficient powers for economic and service regulations to ensure the private companies adhere to the conditions in the agreement set by the government to protect the interests of the consumers. Privatisation will result in enhancing the management and operation of water supply services to be on par with or better than systems in developed countries.

The New Port
A Thriving Channel for Trade

Tan Sri Datuk G. Gnanalingam
Executive Chairman, Kelang Multi Terminal Sdn Bhd

Malaysia today has excellent infrastructure. We not only have the best roads, airports, and the Multimedia Super Corridor, but will also soon be embarking on double-track railways. Malaysia today also has world-class facilities in terms of ports.

Today we have ports and berths that wait for ships rather than vice versa whilst there are still ports in neighbouring areas where ships wait ten days for a berth and a couple of days more to discharge their cargo. For these nations, both capital and inventory are held up at their ports. This scenario was not too unfamiliar five years ago. For a hundred and fifty years, we were quite happy to depend on Singapore to handle all our cargo because Singapore had the capacity, capability, connectivity, certainty and frequency that shipping lines desire. However, with several price increases, it became expensive for Malaysians to do so. When logistics costs become expensive, so does the cost of goods, which will lead to a loss of national competitiveness as compared to emerging countries.

Recognising all these factors, the Government embarked on some key national policies, including:

a) Load centring at Port Klang
b) Building the capacity required
c) Entrusting private sector participation
d) Emphasising productivity and efficiency
e) A zero-inflation policy of low costs

It is truly heartening to see that the Government's policies were not only effectively implemented but also led to revolutionary results within five years. For example:

a) Port Klang's container volume grew from 1.5 million boxes in 1996 to 3.2 million boxes in 2000. In 1980, Port Klang was the 57th largest port in the world. In 1995, it was the 26th. By the year 2000, it had achieved near Top Ten status as the 12th largest port in the world.
b) Westport, which was established in 1996, achieved a million boxes within one thousand days and today handles more than one million boxes per annum.
c) Westport has won many awards, including Asia's Best Terminal, Best Emerging Terminal, the FIABCI Award for Best Public Sector Development and the US Silver Screen Award of promotions.
d) Westport also broke performance standards such as 264 moves per hour for containers, 300 tonnes per hour for Break Bulk and 20,000 tonnes per day for Dry Bulk.
e) The icing on the Malaysian government's policy was Port of Tanjung Pelepas (PTP)'s ability to move one of Singapore's largest customers, which was unthinkable a couple of years ago. PTP is expected to handle 2 million boxes within 2 years.
f) The question arises in many minds as to why all this was not possible before. The answer lies simply in one's capacity and capability to do so. In 1995, Malaysia's port capacity for

> containers was 2 million per year, whilst Singapore's growth alone for the last 5 years was 2 million per year. Singapore's ability to build additional capacity and handle it efficiently attracted all the main line operators to Singapore whilst most Southeast Asian ports remain feeder ports.

Though we have changed the landscape of ports with the desired infrastructure and facilities, we still need to keep abreast of the changing landscape of the industry.

The cargo industry is witnessing the following mega-trends, namely mega-ships, mega-alliances, mega-hubs, mega-networks, and mega-port operators on a mega-highway.

Ships used to carry 2,000 boxes in 1990. This grew to 4,000 boxes in 1995 and 6,000 boxes in the year 2000. Soon, ships will carry 10,000 or 15,000 boxes requiring depths of 15 to 18 metres. Just as many airports are not equipped with runways to handle jumbo-jets, many ports that are not more than 15 metres deep will not be able to handle these ships.

Today, the world is witnessing mega-alliances among the airlines. This trend began with the shipping lines ten years ago such that today six alliances virtually handle 70% of the world's containers. Mega-alliances achieve not only economies of scale but are also efficient in the relay of cargo.

Two decades ago, the major ports of the world were Singapore, Hong Kong, Amsterdam, New York and Los Angeles. Today, we are being supplemented by ports such as Shanghai, Kaohsiung, Gioia Tauro, Pusan, Port Klang, Dubai, Malta, Atlanta and San Diego in San Francisco. Hubs that used to depend on hinterland cargo are now majoring on transshipment cargo.

Through a wave of privatisation in the last decade, six port operators have been able to handle 50% of the world's trade. Major players such as Hutchison and P&O Nedlloyd have developed networks of ports offering standardised Electronic Data Interchange (EDI) systems, network rebates and reliable, world-class services. This dynamic process is a threat to ports run independently, devoid of mega-networking.

In Malaysia today, Westport has partnered the Hutchison Group and is linked globally by shipping alliances that call at Westport. Whilst 15 shipping lines call at Westport, 22 others call at Port Klang to take cargo directly to most destinations in the world. The Government has responded speedily to these developments of globalisation and liberalisation through a multinational ownership of our facilities.

Alliances will jointly determine which ports are most attractive to serve as hubs, basing the decision on location, service and cargo volumes, which in turn drive costs. The mega-hubs and regional hubs potentially will support terminals owned and operated by the leading global operators, and thus could be part of a single EDI network. We will see networks, rather than single ports, having the ability to extract premiums from the value of their network "brand" and this value will be reflected in turn in individual ports. As is the case with airlines, whether you are "in or out" of a key network will impact the value and growth prospects of your port business. This day has not yet arrived. But the trends are emerging, thereby heightening the competitive stakes for ports.

Ports today must provide consistent world-class services and facilities. Speed, efficiency, productivity, consistency—carriers and shippers value these cost-drivers as much as, if not more than, simple port charges. To compete in this environment, ports must invest in the right cranes, loaders, quay expansions and EDI. But investing in equipment and technology alone is not enough.

Service levels and productivity require a commitment on the part of management to develop appropriate processes for using this equipment and then to train and create incentives for staff using the gear.

The strategic partnership with Hutchison will give Westport access to technology, IT systems and productivity ratios at 18 terminals throughout the world. Hutchison owns ports in Myanmar, Indonesia, Hong Kong, China, the Caribbean, Rotterdam and the United Kingdom. There are so many common shipping lines that call at these ports, and they will welcome the benefits of similar IT systems, operating procedures, terminology and productivity.

With the emphasis in this millennium on IT and e-business, Malaysian ports will be the forerunners in this area. Unlike other brick-and-mortar industries that are grappling with this new revolution, the ports have been a click-and-mortar industry for more than three decades. Containerisation has enabled the cargo industry to be digitally operated globally using standardised controls and equipment worldwide. A shipfull of containers is handled by standardised cranes and computer systems worldwide. This development will continue to spearhead efficiencies and economies that cannot be ignored by any port operator. In a just-in-time world, it is fortunate that Malaysia is not devoid of ports to remain competitive as a low-cost producer.

Malaysian Highways

Linking the Nation

Idrose Mohamed
Managing Director, PLUS Bhd

It once took 10 hours to drive from Kuala Lumpur to Penang. The journey wound along what was fondly called the coastal road, and the route, while scenic, was often punctuated by hazards such as potholes and stray livestock.

Now, cars zip up the North-South Expressway (NSE), making the journey in five hours, cruising along well-maintained roads. Anyone wanting a rest or a meal can just pull into the many convenient Rest and Service Areas (RSA) which provide restaurants, restrooms and other amenities. This is the proud achievement of Projek Lebuhraya Utara-Selatan Bhd (PLUS). In fact, the rapid expansion and development of the west coast of Peninsular Malaysia can be attributed to the creation of the PLUS highway which serves as the main artery linking the nation to Thailand in the North and Singapore in the South.

PLUS was set up as the concession company that was given the task of financing, designing, constructing, managing, operating and maintaining the 847.7 kilometres of the NSE, the New Klang Valley Expressway (NKVE) and the Federal Highway Route 2 (FHR2). A wholly-owned subsidiary of United Engineers Bhd, PLUS was incorporated on June 27, 1986. Today, PLUS is recognised as a major service provider in the Malaysian transportation industry, having successfully undertaken the implementation of the single largest privatisation project in the country.

Constructed in phases over a period of seven years, the NSE was officially opened on September 8, 1994, signalling the coming of age of Malaysia's road transport system. The network runs the entire length of the peninsula along its western corridor, from the borders of Thailand in the North to Singapore in the South. The travelling time from Bukit Kayu Hitam (the northernmost point) to Johor Baru (the southernmost extent of the expressway) has been cut by half, to an incredible eight hours.

Other benefits in the form of economic development were perhaps less apparent in the early years but became more and more visible as new townships and industrial parks began to take shape along the length of the expressway and trade and tourism enjoyed a new era of growth.

The NSE is equipped with various facilities to ensure safety and comfort along the way. RSAs are located every 60 kilometres along the expressway and these provide stalls, toilets, showers, public telephones, service stations, wakafs (sheds for resting), parking areas, suraus (prayer rooms) and children's playgrounds. At some RSAs, fast food restaurants and automated teller machines are also provided.

For the safety of motorists using the PLUS-operated highways, the Traffic Monitoring Centre (TMC) operates 24 hours a day to assist with enquiries. The TMC can be reached at 03-26920000. Emergency telephones are located every 2 kilometres along the length of the NSE.

PLUSRonda is a complimentary 24-hour service whereby PLUS vehicles patrol the expressway and provide assistance to motorists who encounter difficulties along the route. For instance, towing to the nearest toll plaza is provided in the event of a major breakdown. Bestowed with auxiliary police powers, PLUSRonda personnel also deal with accidents and general traffic management on the expressway.

PLUS has given much thought to making the drive a pleasant and safe one by landscaping extensively, both along the roads and on the dividers. During the day, the landscape is a pretty sight and at night, the planted dividers limit the light flash from oncoming cars on the other side of the road.

PLUS has also opened Overhead Bridge Restaurants along two points of the expressway, one at Sungai Buloh in Selangor and the other at Ayer Keroh in Malacca. The Overhead Bridge Restaurant across the NSE is linked by a lay-by on either side which provides easy access. There are shoplots, a bridge restaurant, a landscaped car park and amenities such as restrooms with showers and a service station. It is a one-stop RSA with a difference—diners can watch the traffic below them as they dine.

For many Malaysians and visitors, the toll cost is a small price indeed to pay for the safety, ease and comfort of driving on excellent roads.

Putrajaya
Building for Prosperity

Tan Sri Dato' Seri Azizan Zainul Abidin
President, Perbadanan Putrajaya

Malaysia's new Federal Government Administrative Centre, Putrajaya, is the realisation of a vision to build a city capable of meeting the challenges of this millennium. It epitomises the coming of age of Malaysia as an independent and sovereign nation and as a dynamic and progressive member of the global community. Putrajaya is being developed as an intelligent city and a city in a garden within the context of sustainable development.

The proposal to relocate the Federal Government offices out of Kuala Lumpur is not a new idea. It was mooted more than 15 years ago. The underlying objectives are to provide an improved working and living environment and, more particularly, to ease the pressure on Kuala Lumpur's infrastructure. The relocation would give Kuala Lumpur City Hall the opportunity to undertake a review of the city's development and upgrade further its amenities. This would help City Hall realise its objective to turn Kuala Lumpur into Malaysia's commercial and business capital while, at the same time, enhancing its attraction as the Federal Capital.

Furthermore, the relocation of the Federal Government Administrative offices to Putrajaya would result in increased efficiency and productivity through an improved and conducive working environment equipped with the latest technology.

A MODEL OF MALAYSIA INC.

The approach adopted by the Government in the development of Putrajaya is unique. Putrajaya is a showcase of Malaysia Incorporated at its best. It is being developed through a partnership between the private sector and the Government.

Perbadanan Putrajaya, created by an Act of Parliament in 1996, is responsible for the planning, development and management of Putrajaya. Aside from carrying out these responsibilities, it also acts as a local authority and is responsible for providing urban services and local public amenities. Maintenance of the infrastructure, parks and other landscape components will also be the responsibility of Perbadanan Putrajaya. Basically, Perbadanan Putrajaya was created to manage and administer the city for the general wellbeing of the people.

To minimise upfront investment, the physical development of Putrajaya is undertaken by Putrajaya Holdings Sdn Bhd, a company owned by Petronas Bhd (40%), Khazanah Nasional (40%) and the National Heritage Fund (20%). Putrajaya Holdings, as the main developer, is responsible for raising the money required for the construction of Government offices, residential premises and the main infrastructure such as roads, drainage, bridges, the lake and the wetlands.

Kuala Lumpur City Centre Bhd (KLCCB), with its extensive expertise and experience in managing large construction projects, has been appointed the consultant and project manager for both Putrajaya Holdings and Perbadanan Putrajaya.

The major utility companies in the country, namely Tenaga Nasional Bhd, Telekom Malaysia Bhd, Gas Malaysia Bhd and Gas

District Cooling Bhd, have been investing in the development of Putrajaya as part of their business activities.

To date, this formula of teamwork and partnership between the Government and the private sector has proved to be one of the major contributing factors in successfully building Putrajaya in record time.

PUTRAJAYA FACT FILE

Name	Putrajaya, the Federal Government Administrative Centre	
Location	25 km south of Kuala Lumpur, 20 km north of Kuala Lumpur International Airport (KLIA)	
Population	330,000 people	
Total Acreage	4,930 ha	
Land Use (%)	Government	5.3%
	Commercial	2.9%
	Residential	25.8%
	Civic & Cultural	0.2%
	Public Facilities	10.1%
	Utility & Infrastructure	18.2%
	Green Area	37.5%
Development Components	Core Area	1,069.1 ha
	Government Precinct	236.2 ha
	Mixed Development Precinct	55.2 ha
	Civic & Cultural Precinct	35.3 ha
	Commercial Precinct	213.3 ha
	Sports & Recreational	329.1 ha
	Water Bodies, Wetlands & Lake	585.6 ha
	Periphery Area	2,925.3 ha
	Putrajaya Boulevard	100 m wide and 4.2 km long
Transportation Systems	Intracity – monorail, taxi buses	
	Intercity – Express Rail Link, North-South Link	
	KL-Putrajaya-KLIA dedicated highway	
	KL-Seremban Highway	
Phases of Development	Phase 1: 1996-2000	Phase 2: 2000-2005
Implementation	Statutory Authority	Perbadanan Putrajaya
	Developer	Putrajaya Holding Sdn Bhd
	Project Manager	Kuala Lumpur City Centre Bhd

Catalyst for Quality Development

Putrajaya is the largest real estate development in the world. The scale and quality of planning have exerted a tremendous influence on many aspects of Malaysian life. For one, the surrounding areas are benefiting from the massive investment in infrastructure and utilities going into the development of Putrajaya. This is evident in the manifold increase in land value already experienced by these areas.

What is more interesting is that the quality of planning, design work and development in Putrajaya has set new standards and expectations for urban development in Malaysia. Quality, creativity and innovation are the key factors here. This is certainly a step in the right direction for a nation that aspires to be a developed nation by the year 2020.

A Malaysian Identity

One of the greatest challenges in developing Putrajaya is building a city that is identifiably Malaysian. Malaysia is a unique country of diverse cultures and traditions that have merged into a composite culture that is distinctly Malaysian.

The challenge for Perbadanan Putrajaya is to build a city that will be relevant in the future but still rooted in Malaysian culture and traditions. Putrajaya has incorporated the latest in technologies to position the nation to face the future while, at the same time, encouraging values that will help in achieving sustainable development.

The attractive ambience and impressive character of the city is the result of architectural and town-planning efforts directed at creating a harmonious artistic environment with a distinct Malaysian character. The essence of Malaysia can be seen from the grandest buildings to the simplest street fittings in Putrajaya, a national heritage that is being created for future generations.

Community Lifestyle

In the planning of the city, Perbadanan Putrajaya strives to encourage a lifestyle which revolves around a secure, caring and healthy community—strengthened by ties of tradition and a spirit of unity. This approach is very much inspired by the Malaysian traditional *kampung* (village) lifestyle where the wellbeing of the community is the main motivation that drives its members.

One of our objectives is to foster a more pervasive involvement of the residents in activities that would contribute to the enhancement of the community. To achieve this, residential areas in Putrajaya are planned based on a neighbourhood concept where the layout of residential areas and public amenities are designed to encourage greater interaction and foster an abiding sense of neighbourliness among residents. Plazas, squares and recreational areas are essential and integral components of this scheme.

Putrajaya has taken the initiative to break down physical barriers which deter interaction in a community by limiting the erection of high and solid fences around dwelling units. Putrajaya's 'fenceless community' concept is aimed at promoting a caring society that accepts responsibility for the security and wellbeing of the community.

Environment and Sustainable Development

As a city being built on a greenfield site, Putrajaya presents an enormous opportunity for realising a quality living environment and a sustainable human settlement. Right from the outset, the planning of Putrajaya has been entrenched in a Planning Doctrine that places emphasis on the relationship between man and his environment.

This is reflected in the care given to the preservation of natural topography and trees, the control of quality and quantity of storm water and the creation of open space.

BUILDING FOR POSTERITY

Putrajaya is the outcome of a labour of love and a love of nature, culture and people. It reflects Malaysians' growing self-confidence and their aspiration to give expression to their identity. Putrajaya is being built for posterity, a city for this millennium and beyond.

The Property Market Experience

Rising from the Fall

Datuk Eddy Chen Lok Loi
President, Real Estate and Housing
Developers' Association, Malaysia

The onset of the Asian financial crisis in 1997 brought much grief and hardship to the regional economies. The Malaysian housing and property industry was not spared. The shrinkage in demand for properties was only a part of the challenge at that time. The Malaysian property industry also became a prime target for various measures and new guidelines aimed at strengthening the nation's resilience and self-reliance in the face of the economic crisis. After eight years of double-digit growth since 1989, the growth of the sector moderated to 9.5% in 1997 and contracted by 23% and 3.6% in 1998 and 1999 respectively. It was only in the year 2000 that the industry saw a positive, albeit small, upward movement of an estimated 3.1%.

For the Real Estate and Housing Developers' Association (REHDA), fighting for the survival of its members and the industry was a steep, uphill task. The classification of the property industry as a non-productive sector resulting from the over-exposure of banks to property in March 1997, was literally a death sentence on developers. The credit squeeze imposed on new projects that came about six months later practically brought the whole industry to a standstill. It took tireless, continued efforts on the part of the Association to convince the Government that the industry continues to be a significant contributor to the country's economic growth—what with over 140 other subsectors linked to it, upstream and downstream.

As a result of these representations, the Government reclassified housing, especially those in the affordable price bracket of RM250,000 and below, as a productive sector in April 1998, and gave a RM2 billion allocation as financing facilities for low and low-medium-cost housing. This lifted the industry's flagging morale and renewed hopes for a revival of the industry.

REHDA played a further proactive role in highlighting, to the highest levels of the Government, the seriousness of the overhang situation in the property market and its impact on the nation's economic health. Numerous consultations with the relevant authorities ensued, and this resulted in the organisation of the Home Ownership Campaigns.

HOME OWNERSHIP CAMPAIGNS

The first month-long campaign held from December 12, 1998 to January 12, 1999 was fully supported by the Government and offered special incentives to purchasers in the form of discounted prices, waivers of stamp duty and processing fees, reduction in legal fees, higher financing margins, discounts on Mortgage Reducing Term Assurance (MRTA), etc. As a result of these concerted efforts, a total of 19,650 units of properties worth over RM3.6 billion were sold within the one-month campaign.

A second campaign was organised in October 1999. The second campaign saw sales of over 17,578 units of properties worth over RM2.7 billion.

NON-PERFORMING LOANS (NPLS)

A good proportion of the NPLs in the banking system were property-based. Properties are the most common collateral, especially since Malaysian banks have always tended towards collateral lending. Danaharta, the asset management company established in 1998 to take over NPLs from the banking system and expedite loan recovery, had by January 2001, disposed of properties worth over RM487.641 million through its four tender exercises. This represents only about 28% of the indicative value of the properties tendered and this lukewarm interest could be attributed to a still prevalent wait-and-see attitude as well as the non-attractiveness of the price tags attached to the properties.

RISING FROM THE FALL

The Malaysian property market, in going through the crisis, demonstrated that with close consultation and cooperation between the public and private sector in the true spirit of Malaysia Incorporated, a soft landing for the industry could be achieved with minimal devastation to the market. In 1999, as all indicators pointed towards a recovery in the Malaysian economy, the property market improved and projects previously put on hold during the crisis were resumed.

Property developers responded positively and having learned from the crisis, are now more cautious in undertaking new development projects. The days when development projects were initiated based on gut feel and supply pressures were gone and developers are now more analytical in assessing market demand to ensure their products will perform well. Good lessons were learnt, albeit the hard way. Up to the third quarter of 2000, it was reported that 192,720 residential units were completed and 510 new projects were launched for sale. There was much optimism in the market, especially for the affordable housing sector.

There was an urgent need for accurate and timely information on property supply and demand to guide both developers and financial institutions in assessing the viability of projects before funding commitments are made, and the establishment of the National Property Information Centre in 1999 has partially addressed this need.

The huge overhang in other subsectors of the industry, especially purpose-built office and retail complexes, remains the biggest challenge on hand. With average occupancy rates of 77% and 73% respectively, coupled with the incoming additional supply from newly completed buildings, it is envisaged that unless there is a drastic positive upturn of the country's economy, it will take sometime before market demand could catch up with the existing supply of these properties.

With a slowing US economy, we expect there will be some adverse impact on our economy and property market, putting further pressure on our path to sustained recovery. There is still much that needs to be done before we can see a convincing, sustained turnaround. It is now really up to the market players, especially the authorities, financial institutions and private sector developers, to coordinate on planning and working out project viabilities before embarking on any new project so that history will not repeat itself. REHDA will continue to play a leading role in consultations with the authorities on measures to face these challenges.

Cyberjaya
Intelligent Living

Dato' Abdul Karim Abu Bakar
Chief Executive Officer
Setia Haruman Sdn Bhd

Cyberjaya, one of the five designated areas for Multimedia Super Corridor (MSC) status companies, is developing into a world-class intelligent city. The other areas are the Technology Park, UPM Silicon Highway (both located within the MSC), the Petronas Twin Towers and the KL Tower.

Being a cybercity, Cyberjaya is differentiated in terms of the modern, high-tech services it offers while maintaining a high-quality environment and friendly lifestyle for the residents.

Launched by the Prime Minister on May 17, 1997, the Cyberjaya Flagship Zone—the prime phase of Cyberjaya—is already beginning to take shape. Today, there are over 108 companies that have set up their operations in the Flagship Zone amongst which are Fujitsu Systems Business, Telekom Malaysia Bhd, NTT, Microsoft Knowledge Capital Center Sdn Bhd, Nokia (M) Sdn Bhd and British Telecom Multimedia. With the opening of the Multimedia University in June 1999, the working and residential population is now over 7,000.

Apart from the above establishments, Ericsson, Fujitsu, DHL and Tech Linx (a German IT company) are also establishing their IT centres in Cyberjaya.

Developers such as Country Heights Holdings Bhd, Emkay Group and Setia Haruman Sdn Bhd (Setia Haruman) have also commenced their residential developments. The first delivery of completed units to purchasers is expected in the early third quarter of this year.

Along with the city infrastructure, Setia Haruman (the master developer of Cyberjaya Flagship Zone) has also been providing office spaces. Apart from the fully occupied 120,000 sq. ft. of office space in Cyberview Lodge and Cyberview Gardens office complexes, Century Square, with a total area of 500,000 sq. ft. of space, is ready for occupancy. Blocks 1 and 2 are fully occupied whilst Blocks 3 and 5 are 60% and 70% booked. In addition, another 470,000 sq. ft. of office space is expected to be completed by the end of 2001.

It is envisaged that by 2011, the Cyberjaya Flagship Zone will be a bustling city with a population of approximately 120,000.

INTELLIGENT TOWNSHIP

Cyberjaya has become the ideal test-bed for innovative ideas and new technologies.

Various infrastructure such as roads and networks, drainage and sewerage systems, utilities such as water, electricity, gas district cooling and telecommunication facilities have been progressively planned and constructed. Public amenities such as smart schools and Phase 1 of the 500-acre Cyber Park will be completed by the end of 2001 while the mosque, police and fire stations are scheduled to be completed by 2003.

Setia Haruman feels that a model intelligent city must be different in terms of lifestyle for the residents as well as the business community. An intelligent city must also be efficient and effective in the overall management of the city services. Those who live and work in Cyberjaya must have inexpensive and ubiquitous access to a broad range of modern information and communication resources to conduct their businesses and social activities, as well as to enhance their quality of life.

Setia Haruman has set up a special team to strategise the transformation of traditional developments into a high-tech city. Several key ideas were conceived and put to the test. Today, Cyberjaya has plans to provide broadband networks, both wired and eventually wireless, to give high-speed, high-capacity access for massive voice, data and multimedia delivery. Office and commercial buildings and residential developments will have fibre access and cabling infrastructure where businesses and residents can readily access the Internet and obtain a multitude of services from it, as well as from the World Wide Web. Television shows will be broadcast without the unsightly antenna using the broadband network. The high bandwidth will be ideal for the eventual offering of video-on-demand applications. A pilot broadband and video-on-demand system is already being offered to buildings and residential developments in Cyberjaya.

The Sepang District Office, being the local authority for Cyberjaya, will enjoy the most advanced online city management system. An online digital map of the Cyberjaya Flagship Zone along with a complete database of its assets and residents will be made available to facilitate more effective management of the city.

CITY COMMAND CENTRE

These ideas are being implemented via a special project called the City Command Centre which provides the single hub for integration and distribution of various services. This is the first attempt in the world to provide a wide range of community and city management services under one roof that is able to generate revenue and be self-sustaining when critical mass is reached.

All major junctions with signals will be equipped with closed circuit television cameras, advanced video imaging technology and an adaptive traffic management system to intelligently control traffic lights and provide visual surveillance to ensure smooth traffic flow with minimal congestion. The city will have a portal providing real-time travel information such as traffic news, car park information, places of interest, city maps and directions, travel planner and so forth.

Various buildings and even homes can be remotely monitored to ensure they are safe and secure. In office complexes, the fire alarms, security, air-conditioning systems, lifts, car parks, lighting, power, sanitary and other building services can be monitored on real-time. Building owners can reduce their operations and management staff, especially after office hours, and yet be assured that their buildings are fully managed. Homes, especially multi-tenanted condominiums or apartment complexes, can have similar options where their security and home automation systems can be remotely connected to the City Command Centre. Most important, the utility services are also monitored to ensure that the highest level of service is provided in line with the MSC bill of guarantees.

A community portal is being implemented where the residents can obtain up-to-date community news and current happenings in Cyberjaya. The bulletin board offers a platform for residents to post messages to one another and a platform for electronic discussion. Each resident may opt for his own e-mail account which is linked to a private mailbox for voice mail and facsimile—a unique and cost-effective offering for start-up companies, home business or personal use. Eventually, by working closely with major banks, the Cyberjaya community portal will have a range of e-commerce services such as bill enquiry and payment, shopping, auction, education, and of course, direct access to the World Wide Web.

The Sepang District Office will also enjoy a suite of application systems to assist them in the billing and collection of assessment, the online booking of public facilities such as badminton, squash and tennis courts, multi-purpose halls, etc. as well as online application and issuance of licences.

INTELLIGENT OFFICE BUILDINGS

Occupants of office complex buildings demand a multitude of services and building owners must carefully plan them right at the inception stage. Architects and engineers have to take into account the design of an IT-ready building. A vast amount of broadband and capacity must be available for voice, data and video services.

Setia Haruman has tried innovative ideas in the Cyberview Lodge and Gardens. Within these complexes, the office suites comprise small stand-alone single or double-storey buildings offering a private and conducive environment for creative minds. Each unit is wired for both telephone and data services. Tenants are provided with extension telephones complete with individual private numbers. The campus network available to each unit also provides immediate high-speed Internet access. In fact, Cyberview Lodge has PCs with Internet access in each and every one of their chalets and suites, a rare offering even in most advanced countries.

Tenants of Century Square also enjoy the above facilities, apart from the in-house telephone system and data network. The building can be remotely monitored from the City Command Centre where common services such as lifts, air-conditioning, lighting, security, car parks, electricity and plumbing can be controlled. Tenants can lodge a complaint or reserve certain facilities available for booking by telephone or via Internet access.

A guideline is being prepared for other developers to conform to building office complexes with intelligent features. This is to meet high-tech, communications and multimedia businesses' demand for such high-quality office spaces and broadband access.

Smart Homes

Smart homes consist of more than just gadgets controlling lighting and appliances. Manufacturers are now producing Web-enabled electronic consumer appliances. Once "wired-up" and using simple Web-based applications, home owners can remotely manage their homes via the telephone and Internet.

Residential developments in Cyberjaya will have the benefit of broadband access. The convergence of broadcasting, communication and computer by the Internet allows Cyberjaya to explore distribution not only through the existing terrestrial television channels but also other multimedia contents via the broadband access. Internet-ready homes with high speed broadband access will be likened to living on the information superhighway.

In North America, cable television providers are using their cable networks to provide high speed Internet access. Without inheriting older copper, coaxial or hybrid fibre coaxial networks, Cyberjaya is able to leapfrog to the latest and most advanced broadband network using Asynchronous Transfer Mode. With such ambitious plans, fibre optic networks must be installed throughout Cyberjaya to provide the links between the hub and the customers' premises. Developers must also pre-wire the commercial buildings and residential units to take advantage of such offerings.

Smart School

In the development of Cyberjaya, Setia Haruman will also be providing a smart school. Smart School, one of MSC's flagship applications, is being implemented in stages nationwide. To support the nation's Vision 2020, the smart school's initiative will create a new generation of Malaysians—Malaysians who are more creative and innovative in their thinking, adept in new technologies, and able to access and manage completely the information explosion.

Cyberjaya's Smart School will be constructed by Setia Haruman as part of public amenities and this school is to be equipped with the most advanced infrastructure. This IT infrastructure supports the new way of teaching, learning and management processes and provides connectivity to the external constituencies and the educational network with other smart schools locally and internationally. With the high bandwidth access available only in Cyberjaya, this Smart School will have a powerful superhighway to a resource bank for teacher training materials, electronic curriculum for students, technical support, and other information.

E-COMMERCE

The world is moving towards virtual shopping, electronic commerce and integrated marketing. In Cyberjaya, the community portal, cyberjaya.com.my provides the "shop front" and linkages to e-commerce for residents and visitors.

In the current plan, utility companies will be able to electronically present the latest bills to their customers. The residents will receive automatic reminders and will find it convenient to pay their bills by just clicking a few buttons on their keyboards or at the kiosks provided by the City Command Centre at strategic locations. Residents can even preset auto payment instructions so that their bank accounts are automatically deducted to pay various utilities and other types of bills.

Most important in making e-commerce successful is the payment system. Most banks in Malaysia already offer electronic banking which can be easily linked to the *cyberjaya.com.my* community portal. Once such payment systems exist, more merchants, contractors and suppliers can register their services online to attract business from residents.

Conclusion

The construction industry is under pressure to adapt to the changes brought by IT. Expertise in IT is now required from the planning and design team so that whole townships, office buildings and even residential homes are not isolated from the new wave of computing and communication.

Competition is no longer just about price or location, but the IT readiness of the property. Cyberjaya, being the first intelligent city, is the platform to create a working model for future cities. The IT readiness of buildings and homes will enable electronic services and e-commerce to be brought to the desktops of residential and commercial units.

Security & International Relations

Defence

Preparing for all Contingencies

Dato' Sri Mohd Najib Tun Razak
Minister, Ministry of Defence

The end of the cold war has brought about both dangers and opportunities, just like the Chinese characters describing crisis. As the dust is yet to settle down, we are still in a state of flux, as the strategic environment is in the process of evolution. It is clear from our experience that during such times, we need to prepare ourselves and ensure that we are in a position to meet a whole range of contingencies, covering not only military threats, but also non-military elements. After all, with globalisation, with the primacy of external environment, we have little choice but to look beyond our borders for today these are being ripped apart, making them at times, irrelevant. Therefore, in such an age, we have to keep all our options open and as the saying goes, "prepare for the worst and hope for the best."

Within the ambit of security and defence, Malaysia has adopted several approaches. While being engaged in the global arena, for instance, by participating in the United Nations peacekeeping operations, we have been active in the Asia-Pacific region. Here, we not only take part in regional multilateral security and defence frameworks, such as the Asean Regional Forum (ARF) and the Five

Powers Defence Arrangements (FPDA), we have also established intricate linkages involving bilateral military relations. This open policy of establishing ties has indeed enhanced our national and regional security.

At the end of the day, we need to rely on our own strength, our national resilience, and this falls on the shoulders of our security forces as well as the citizens of the country. Ever since Independence, the Malaysian armed service is a professional military force. With this unblemished record on being apolitical, military defence is the sole responsibility of the Malaysian Armed Forces (MAF). The MAF guarantees the territorial integrity of the country. Like most armed forces, its development was influenced by the evolution of the nation. As the country faced an internal threat, based on ideology, there was an urgent need for the MAF to contain and defeat armed communism. While the fight started in 1948, it was only in December 1989 that the communists finally capitulated.

The long struggle had resulted in the MAF being an imbalanced force. Beginning in the late 1980s, Malaysia began to embark on a modernisation programme that is to transform the MAF into a conventional force, having the capability to meet such threats. This has several elements, namely, a restructuring which would reflect a much more tri-service orientation; a doctrinal shift, emphasising on joint and combined operations; and the acquisition of military assets that are much more sophisticated in order to meet the conventional requirements of the armed forces.

Deterrence has been at the core of our defence philosophy. Over time, this concept has been proven to be effective. However, we know that for deterrence to work, it has to be credible. The worst kind of deterrence is when one is falsely deceiving oneself.

In this respect, we continue to upgrade not only assets, but also our men. The relationship between man and machine has existed throughout the ages. We recognise that while machines can be replaced, man is indispensable. In this respect, we continue to emphasise the welfare and the wellbeing of our soldiers, seamen and airmen.

Today, with the emergence of all kinds of possible scenarios, the MAF is preparing itself to meet the whole spectrum of threats, from low intensity to high intensity conflicts. This poses a myriad of challenges to the three services. However, the bottom line is that we need to prepare ourselves, for when the balloon goes up and the chips are down, our armed forces are ready to engage the enemy, to overwhelm him and to be victorious. This, after all, is what the business of war is all about. *Si vis pacem para bellum*—for peace prepare for war.

Malaysia has enjoyed almost uninterrupted peace for nearly forty-five years. This has been achieved through the prudent leadership that we have since Independence. To us, defending Malaysia goes beyond mere military. It is multi-faceted, covering from economic wellbeing to societal and political stability. Our economic policy of an equitable distribution of wealth has been the hallmark of the country's development. We need to continuously raise the stakes amongst Malaysians as a way to guarantee a policy of 'prosperity for all.' After all, it is us who will end up defending Malaysia, no one else.

Foreign Policy
Developing Partnerships for Peace and Prosperity

Dato' Seri Syed Hamid Jaafar Albar
Minister, Ministry of Foreign Affairs

At the dawn of the new millennium, the world is in the throes of the most rapid period of change ever in history. Paradigms are constantly falling. Concepts of national security, for example, were largely premised upon defence assets and strategic alliances. Today, national security must encompass a wider range of concerns. We have already seen how capital can be manipulated to impoverish and destabilise nations and regions. Globalisation also poses new challenges to our wellbeing and our ability to achieve national goals.

Information Technology has truly transformed the world into a global village. An isolated event in Kuala Lumpur instantly becomes the subject of discussion in the remotest parts of the world, thanks to global television and the Internet. Views are shaped and opinions formed in an instant. The global media is no longer merely a witness of events but an active and often biased shaper of opinion. Perception becomes reality and takes on a life of its own. Governments must often compete with non-state actors, even a lone crusader with access to a modem, to tell their story, defend their actions or promote a cause.

There has also been an increasing tendency to exploit issues like human rights, labour conditions and environmental concerns to further disadvantage developing countries. We recognise that these are important issues and that it is the desire for people everywhere to live in freedom and dignity and in a safe and healthy environment. The Government of Malaysia fully supports these aspirations and reflects them in its national agenda. However, these issues have been consistently exploited by developed countries to seek commercial and political advantage. Hence, they censure one country for its lack of democracy while continuing to pander to other countries where there is not even a modicum of democracy because it is in their national or commercial interests to do so!

The world has therefore changed and diplomacy must change with it. Foreign ministries all over the world should rise to face these new challenges. In an effort to understand and respond to increasingly complex and multifaceted trends, diplomats have to acquire new skills and forge new partnerships with businessmen, bankers, environmentalists and engineers, to name a few.

To thrive in the new millennium, our foreign policy must be based on the philosophy of finding common cause with others and building partnerships for peace and prosperity. Such partnerships will strengthen our ability to maintain our independence and our sovereignty and help us to pursue our national interests in a world where power—economic, political and financial as well as that derived from new technologies—is becoming increasingly monopolised by a few nations and unhesitatingly used to secure unfair advantages in almost every sphere of human activity. Enhancing cooperation and building partnerships must therefore be the hallmarks of our foreign policy.

Within this overall framework of building partnerships, there are a number of concentric circles of interest that will be Malaysia's focus. Firstly, we will need to pay special attention to the global financial architecture to ensure that our economy is not disadvantaged. We will also need to closely monitor and influence emerging global trade and commercial trends so that we will continue to have the best possible environment for our exports while remaining a competitive destination for foreign investments. Globalisation has the potential to inundate us and we ignore at our own peril.

Secondly, we will need to ensure that our region continues to remain peaceful and stable. Recent developments have demonstrated how easy it is for others to impose their own agendas on the region when economies are weakened and national resilience undermined. Asean is the bedrock of regional stability and therefore strengthening Asean cohesiveness will be a major priority.

There is also quite a clear appreciation that East Asia must evolve new mechanisms for cooperation and partnership to meet global and regional challenges. Regional initiatives such as an Asian monetary fund and other measures to protect our economies from destabilising trends must be pursued. East Asia must also strive to bring to bear our combined economic and political weight to protect our common interests. An East Asia that learns to work together and is dependent upon each other for trade, investment and growth will also have great reason to avoid destablising actions. Unless this process of regional cooperation and partnership succeeds, we will always be at a disadvantage. Asean has shown the way and it must now find the consensus to underpin this wider regional concert.

No attempt at building partnerships would be complete without closer cooperation with other developing countries. The majority of the nations of the world fall into this category of 'developing countries.' There is strength in numbers. Their success is our success and consequently, their marginalisation would weaken us also. There can also be little hope of trying to create a more balanced and equitable global architecture without greater cooperation and solidarity amongst developing countries. Together we can help defend and advance our common interests. Of course, to be effective, developing countries must create more effective mechanisms for cooperation and coordination. We will work with other countries of the South to achieve this.

We also have in the 'Ummah' as exemplified by the OIC, a natural partnership of nations cemented by our shared religious beliefs. However, the OIC must not remain merely a gathering of fraternal countries bound by a common religion. It must become a force for change, for unity, for justice, for progress, and for the advancement of science and technology in the world. Together, we can march forward in a new partnership for peace and progress.

Of course, the emphasis on Asia and the developing world does not mean that we will neglect other regions. We have important and mutually beneficial relations with Europe and America as well and we want to maximise these relations. There is, however, a need to redefine and renew our partnership with the United States and Europe. We want a partnership based on mutual benefit and mutual respect.

Finally, there is our partnership with the United Nations (UN). Although we are a small nation, we have been unflinching in our efforts to develop a strong partnership with the UN in the struggle to establish more equitable global rules and strengthen peace and stability. We have ardently supported international efforts to protect the victims of aggression and genocide in Asia, Africa, West Asia and Europe, contributing troops for UN peacekeeping efforts as well as providing other types of assistance. However, the UN is often hindered by its own structures that allow a few member states to use the UN for their own interests. If we are to have a UN that is more responsive to the needs of its members, reform is necessary. We will therefore work with other like-minded countries to help restructure the UN to serve our collective interests better.

Malaysia has demonstrated in recent years that if we are united and determined to safeguard our national interest, there is no force in the world that can deter us. Though the new millennium brings new challenges, I am confident that we can build new partnerships for peace and prosperity that will enable us to achieve cherished national goals and a better life for all our citizens.

Social

Wearing the Malaysian Hat

Whose Youth, What Forum?

Dr Shafiq Sit Abdullah
Director & CEO
APEC's Partnership for Equitable Growth and
Chairman, Asia News Broadcasting and ANB Group

Someone once said that our privileges in life should never outweigh our obligations and responsibilities. If we subscribe to this basic tenet, then wearing the Malaysian hat should be quite a privilege for most Malaysians. Ironically, however, many young Malaysians would disagree with this. Some have even come to assume that privileges are birth rights.

Youth specialists, academic experts and politicians have tried to explain this as a general characteristic of the young, of the restless, of the idealist needing space to realise high hopes and dreams. The youth remain unconvinced. Reformasi further complicated matters and saw a fractured Malaysian political consensus especially among the youth. Some have begun to question which hat, if any at all, should be worn for the betterment of our country.

At the outset, let me say that the notion that any other hat could be worn and mean more to any Malaysian, young or old, escapes the author. In part, the deterioration in our country's social fabric and unity stems as much from the success of the New Economic Policy (NEP) as from its failure to address the longer term interest of our nation. As the youth become more educated and better informed, they will increasingly question why. Coupled with the underlying belief that this country is stable enough to take some abuse over whatever they are unhappy about, some youths have made the choice to question authority. In a sense, the country becomes a victim of its own success.

This, however, does not explain the abrasive manner in which some youths are questioning why and taking to the streets. At one level, the unfamiliar arrogance and untimely breakdown in the Malay-anchored *peramah* attitudes of Malaysians can be attributed to problems arising from the implementation of the NEP. But then again, there are a hundred and one other reasons (including the role of parents and maybe too much chocolates) as to why we have failed to cultivate values such as gratitude and tolerance. Pushed also by the tide of Western influence and MTV where children and pop icons call their parents by their first names, many young Malaysians have become confused in their sensibilities, if not adrift in their values.

Today, the youth assume that it is their right that certain privileges like a good education, freedom and clean toilets are accorded to them. In part, we can also blame this on the way the NEP was implemented—with many young graduates believing that the hand-out system is the way to go. Life is meant to be easy with no hard work required, spoon feeding a norm rather than a short period of assistance to level the playing field. Privileges become seen as rights where no obligations are expected in return.

Other discerning youth, rich or poor, read between the lines in newspapers. The central fourth estate then becomes mistakenly seen as a mouthpiece in a funny Shakespearian tragedy. This fortifies the youth's sense of belief that they are no different than Jim Carrey in *The Truman Show*, and that in their opinion, rightly or wrongly, there is little they can do to make a difference. This belief is potentially dangerous and has led many youths to join opposition parties or worse still, to take to the streets such that their mirror in society, the press, reflects the angry image of themselves on print trying to make a difference. In a perverse manner, this outlet brings contentment to some youths who unfortunately give little regard to the impact it has on foreign direct investment through the international press.

As a young nation, we know we have to reward achievement, hard work and honesty, deter laziness and punish dishonesty. But in practice, it seems that there is a discrepancy. For the idealistic youth, dishonesty in many forms is apparent in our society. From the act of taking a gold coin as a souvenir item to using one's position of power to enhance one's wealth and standing in society, it is clear that such practice is disdained upon quietly and is intrinsically unstable.

Judging from the results of the last election, it is clear that our youth are impatient for change. Driving through Malaysia then, I sensed a mood among the youth that they feel strongly that, for example, corruption is destroying the nation.

Not surprisingly, coffee shop talk among the youth centres around how the police is giving them a tough time for riding their bikes without mufflers, while not doing enough to curb, for example, white-collar crimes or rape in Malaysia. To be sure, one can never satisfy the caped crusader in the youth or the skewed idealistic perception of young individuals, many of whom may not have really worked for a living. But this has always been the case, and not just of late. So what has changed?

One explanation sits uncomfortably at both extremes of the spectrum of Malaysian life. On the one hand, religion-based politics have begun systematically to exploit discontentment of the youth. PAS, for example, has focused on filling the void in the youth's life, even in distant shores where our youth are sent for further studies.

Instead of broadening their horizons in life, the youth return to their kampungs as men of science, advising their folks on the wrong-doings of the government. Little if any consideration is given to the hard work of others and the policies of the government that have provided for their education and wellbeing.

On the other end of the spectrum, materialism has made its way into our culture. The importance placed on wealth has fuelled greed and other vices. Not surprisingly, some now think that they should have a piece of the action. This applies also to those who have cleverly worked a way around Ali Baba schemes to exploit the NEP.

To be sure, idealism is a trait of all youth and fighting what some may deem as corruption is a strong symbol of idealism. The rebel without a cause is also a natural hero for the youth. Still, this acknowledgement should not be used as a passport for bad behaviour. Our youth are not only challenging the assumptions which once made wearing a Malaysian hat meaningful. Many are questioning the issues of right and wrong, and that wearing the Malaysian hat need not necessarily mean being of a similar mind and soul to the ruling coalition's campaign slogans. This is all fine and dandy. The point, however, that many youths are missing is that it is not at all clear whether the outcomes in our country are void of foreign influence or intervention. Whether or not in the youth's idealistic quest for greater democracy, they will secure an outcome actually pre-ordained by our competitors.

It would be naive if all our youth believed that, for example, the Asian economic crisis was the outcome of domestic issues.

Domestically, some of this has taken place. The fine balance between order and justice seems to have taken a tilt. The new catch phrase of justice and the free Anwar campaign appear to have taken a grip on some of our youth. Incredibly enough, some of the ruling elite seem to have bought into their own propaganda that this grip is unimportant and that time will work everything out. How critically wrong. Time is in fact the culprit here. The youth are young and young people tend to remember silly things.

Concurrently and underlying the mood today is also a sense that it matters what race we belong to. This mood is unhealthy. It leads to the youth believing there is a contradiction between being patriotic and what religious hat the citizen should wear. In practice, it should not matter whether the Malaysian is a good Muslim, Christian, Buddhist or Hindu. The multiplicity of religious beliefs and the underlying respect and tolerance of the differences is what makes Malaysia great and uniquely special.

To make matters worse, there are youth groups today who have decided that the best way to counter extremism is to be equally extreme. This has caused further confusion in the minds of the young. Clearly, political groups which go on a bandwagon espousing fanatic racial ideals have never stood the test of time.

As a developing country, the authorities have rightly tried to prevent debate on nation-building issues which could be sensitive to racial harmony. This, however, has not worked as polarisation among the races continues. Constructive debate among the youth should be encouraged gradually to cultivate an ability to appreciate and better manage racial sensitivities in the context of nation-building issues. Over time, the youth should be allowed to clarify any misunderstandings and demonstrate a quiet confidence in an ability to disagree knowledgeably. Genuine efforts to help build our maturity of thought should be lauded. For example, ANB's enlightening TV programme, *Dateline Malaysia*, generated such discourse and remains a great effort in this direction.

Why else should one wear a Malaysian hat if, at the end of the day, the hat only obscures our vision and thinking? The youth also seem to understand that the leaders of tomorrow need to be respected. Respect has to be earned through a willingness to work hard and excel in their respective fields of endeavour, professional or otherwise.

Mediocrity has, however, seeped its way into our culture. It is not a crime to be stupid, but it is definitely a mistake to aspire to be stupid or mediocre. Blame this also on the poor implementation of the NEP? The implementation of most things will have an effect since every action should have a similar but opposite reaction. If so, then we have to address urgently the wrong belief that it is who you know that counts, not what you know. The way forward for the youth must be to inculcate another set of beliefs, that is, how best one needs to put into practice what one knows to move ahead in life. Study more and network politics less. Otherwise, the Malay dilemma will be so firmly anchored in our youth's psyche that it will be impossible to dislodge in the new global knowledge society.

Once the acceptance of mediocrity sets into the mindset and culture of a nation, it becomes a mathematical certainty that the downward slide will begin. For the educated youth, many will forget about becoming world-class. One can easily get a back door into the Oxford and Harvard alumni by attending a short management course. Not that such alumni should be given great importance. The point is that we have to think for ourselves, and it really does not matter where one receives formal education, if at all any. A personal observation: creative thinking and formal education seldom go together. This handicap has not for example deterred me from writing, reading or producing a film in a studio. Whatever it is, it is important that we try our best.

Sometimes we want to believe that the world owes us a living and that success is assured. In reality, there are no guarantees. The 1997 economic contagion proved this. To stay ahead, we relied on ourselves, our conviction and our abilities. Can we imagine what Malaysia would be like today if we could not think for ourselves then? The ringgit peg, with its accompanying stability reinforces this appreciation for self-sufficiency. Hard work, prudence and the values of our forefathers should be revisited.

Liberal writers would say that it is the youth's responsibility to question why and to be rebellious. It is expected of them. In any case, compared to the highly ferocious youth in South Korea and elsewhere, foreign observers have commented that our youth look like poodles in a park. Such comments made matters worse, as our youth then strove to overcompensate and become fierce poodles on the street, with little regard for the rule of law and the proper constitutional way to address their grievances—through the ballot box.

It is not so much that many of our youth seem to believe that a greater opposition to the ruling government is necessarily a good thing. But it is clear that many are drifting, somewhere between the old language of raising the Malaysian flag and removing the Union Jack, and the new uncertainties. Maybe in this day and age, it has become untenable to think that any youth in his or her right mind would spend more than a minute a day thinking about King and country. This apathy is perhaps not intentional but nonetheless most harmful. So the good news is, at least, we know that our youth are passionate about the future of our nation, however misguided some of them may be.

Some believe that the lack of contentment has arisen because of the widening communication gap between students and the government. The initiative to form the National Students Consultative Council (NSCC) to bridge the gap is a step in the right direction. The issues, aspirations and achievements of the youth, however, can only be addressed through action and less talk. Already, the youth seem to think that it is more worthwhile subscribing to something nebulous like human rights, than good old-fashioned patriotism. Such a preference among the youth is OK provided the country, especially a developing country, has matured thinking citizenry. In this light, it becomes compelling then that as a nation we will have to encourage dialogue, debate and through the discourse, build understanding, teamwork and greater unity.

Fortunately, the youth understand that every nation needs good leadership, which in turn requires an equally good team to deliver the promises. Broken promises to constituents are the best way to destroy national consensus. The citizenry by and large, works hard, pays taxes and expects the government to deliver. When their hard work is not rewarded with good management and results, they vote with their feet and choose the alternative. As such, it is crucial that emphasis is given to quality, discourage mediocrity, get the best batters in the team to build the conditions for a strong rallying cry, and through them, the foundation for great teamwork and unity.

At the core of unity is the need for the youth to see tolerance as a value. Tolerance is central and should be cultivated among the races and income groups if we truly intend to maintain social and national cohesion. As the pressures of globalisation continue to pull at the seams of our country from all corners, this task will become more difficult over time. The youth thus rely on the government to promote tolerance and better understanding among the races. The youth depend also on religious authorities to help widen the religious consensus and restrict the extremists from making religion an unsightly battleground for something as mundane as politics.

So as we ask the youth to cling on to the Malaysian hat, we need to ask ourselves the question: Why should the youth listen and be obedient in their response to this request? They look around and see public officials having celebrity wives and all the trappings of power. In the minds of the idealistic youth, the maths do not add up. Simple addition tells them that the salary packages of these officials cannot possibly afford them such a lifestyle. The youth logically feel that something is amiss. Why should I wear a Malaysian hat when the people I am supposed to look up to do not, or worse still, are wearing imported items? The caped crusader in their aspirations to "change the world and make it a better place" re-emerges.

Finally, the youth yearn for respect. The youth are particular about being treated as adults and as equals. How can you achieve this in a society where we have special car parks for cars with special badges attached to special number plates. It is really quite ludicrous, and even sadder, that it has permeated our social consciousness: that there are people out there buying single-digit number plates to appear to be in the same circle of VIPs. Even better still, stick a shiny looking emblem on the number plate to make it look like a Minister's car—sometimes in jest, sometimes to challenge the authority of the law: everyone is equal in the eyes of the law. "So how come the Minister and aristocrat have a better car park slot?" says the unknowing youth, reaching out tentatively for her hat.

In closing, if we are serious about wearing the Malaysian hat, then we will have to stake our claim and our ownership of the hat, and not leave it adrift, not knowing where the youth of our country belong, and whose forum they should really be representing. Until then, the current fractured consensus will continue to irk our youth's idealistic quest for utopia, and for a perfect Malaysia. But, as alluded to earlier, Malaysia does not exist as an island in deep space. There are factors that are beyond our ambit of influence, which, unfortunately, have a direct impact on our livelihoods. I say this with my Malaysian hat on, even though my work constituency is a wider regional forum.

For its part, the youth need to understand that idealism must be tempered with the right dose of realism, and that youthful exuberance be balanced with time-tested patience. It is critical to know that if we choose not to wear a Malaysian hat, then we are actually not wearing another, unknowingly, which is detrimental to the development of our nation. Alternatively and arguably easier, since some youths have become so accustomed to such a way, we could make an open admission that Malaysians do not wear hats and be done with it.

Sports

Providing the Playground for World-Class Events

Tunku Imran Tuanku Ja'afar
President, Olympic Council of Malaysia

From the time Malaysia (then Malaya) inaugurated its Independence on August 31, 1957 with the Merdeka soccer tournament, the country has steadily built up a reputation for the skilled organisation of sports events. Though that tournament was not a world-class event—it drew its field from South and East Asian teams—it marked a remarkable first: it was the world's first invitational event in which the host paid the expenses for all participants. It was held in a spanking new stadium, fittingly called Merdeka (Independence) Stadium. Sir Stanley Rous, then President of soccer's world governing body FIFA, was amazed that a newly independent nation could bring off such an event. Rous' admiration for the man behind the idea and its success—Tunku Abdul Rahman, the country's founding premier—was said to be the sort children normally accord the conjuror who pulls out silk handkerchiefs from a hat at some point during a birthday party.

More than four decades since that remarkable beginning, Malaysia is now seen to be a country with a formidable array of sports infrastructure. No sleight of hand was required to construct the facilities Malaysia now has that can host world-class sports events; the hard currency that went into building this multibillion-ringgit sports infrastructure came on the back of buoyant economic growth recorded in a robust decade starting from the late 1980s. The decision of the Commonwealth Games Federation in 1992 to award the 16th Games in the series to Malaysia was the spur for the construction of an array of stadia and arena for the multi-disciplinary Games in Kuala Lumpur in 1998. Outside of Japan, China, Thailand and South Korea, Malaysia is about the only Asian country to have the full range of facilities needed to host an Olympic Games. Malaysia vied with a slew of other countries to host the 2008 Olympic Games. But the bid failed in the first round. Realistically, we stood little chance of getting past the first round of the evaluation process. But observers noted that entering the bid was important to the future prospects of a country attempting to bid for the Games.

No doubt, Malaysia's prospects of hosting an event like the Olympic Games were dented by our failure to succeed in our first bid to host the 2006 Asian Games. Malaysia ran a dispiriting second to rival Qatar in the bid that was put to the vote in an Olympic Council of Asia (OCA) meeting in Pusan on November 12, 2000. But failure at Pusan was attributed to factors other than infrastructural readiness and organisational competence. In the latter two aspects, Malaysia was widely seen as superior to its rivals for the bid. Now the Olympic Council of Malaysia's strategy for keeping Malaysia in the sporting world's eye is to bid for and host single-discipline world, continental and regional sports events so that our in-place facilities would be periodically used, refurbished and upgraded. That way we can serve up the country's merits as a world-class playground for the various sporting disciplines to the world bodies whose high opinion of our facilities and expertise must ultimately count in the evaluations of the International Olympic Committee (IOC) and

OCA when it comes to selecting the host nation for their quadrennial Games.

If, at the beginning of Malaysia's quest for international recognition as a capable host of sports events, our strengths leaned towards soccer, field hockey and badminton, in recent years, while maintaining our prowess in these disciplines, we have diversified our capabilities to include golf, shooting, table-tennis, cycling and even, perhaps most famously of all, Formula One racing. The accoutrements required for the hosting of world golf and Formula One events place a high premium on first-class and plentiful hotel accommodation, high-tech communications facilities, a commodious international airport and enticing tourist resorts. A world-class motor racing track and an acclaimed golf course together with the aforementioned props complete the array of facilities the nation's capital of Kuala Lumpur has within a 40-kilometre radius south of the city. Few nations in the world have this concentration of multifarious facilities within one area as Malaysia does. Within this area, stage and props unite with function to such advantageous effect, as was seen in the last two years when Malaysia hosted one leg of the Formula One Grand Prix for cars and the World Cup Golf for teams. The world's best drivers and golfers came, competed and relaxed in splendid environs.

Increasingly, in the recent past, Malaysia has become the venue not just for high-profile sports events in golf and motor racing, but also for newfangled ones like climbing and carroms. This attests to our propensity for event organisation and also to the availability of facilities. Additional reasons for the popularity of the country as a venuc for sports and other events are the friendliness of the Malaysian people and the variety of its cuisine. The cosmopolitanism of the people and food and the fact that the country has large areas of refreshingly green foliage are objects of fascination to foreigners. Several races live together in peace and mutual accommodation, adding to the general atmosphere of amity and wellbeing, making the country a cynosure.

However, if the likes of Tiger Woods and Mika Hakkinen came, saw and were enticed, they may not have been charmed by what may have seemed to many as a paucity of sports culture in Malaysia. This would refer to the shortage of a sports ethos in the nation, a cultural understanding that permeates a country like Australia where nearly the entire citizenry is conversant not only with the argot of whichever sport they happened to be following, but also its decorum. Sure, Australia is seen as a developed country while Malaysia, despite its remarkable economic strides that saw impressive rises in its per capita income in the 1990s, is still striving to enter that category. Though in Malaysia, there is considerable coordination among the Sports Ministry, National Sports Council, OCM and its affiliates, a vital force for the dissemination of a sporting culture is still unaware of its centrality to the effort. This is the Education Ministry. To be sure, this ministry does do its considerable part in promoting sports in its extra-curricular programmes. But this promotion only affects the sports-inclined, not the entire body of the school population, large numbers of whom may not know the difference between a golf club and a hockey stick. The insemination of an ethic of sports understanding into the core curriculum in schools is a long way from conception, let alone implementation. A start has to be made, otherwise unaware Malaysians will still continue to chatter on the golf course when a player is addressing a putt and boo when an opposing team in field hockey takes a penalty corner. Such indecorous behaviour does not match the splendour of the infrastructure that Malaysia has in place to stage world events, nor does it raise the esteem of a nation that aspires to accompany the ambition to stage world events with the yen to excel at performing in them.

In tandem with the insertion of sports into the core curriculum in schools, it would greatly help the education of the citizenry in sports if a television channel were devoted entirely to sports. In recent years, Malaysians have witnessed the proliferation of television channels for their entertainment and edification. But one locally-based channel devoted to sports was not among the innovations. It is time such a sports channel is introduced so that corporate and other sponsors, sports fans and the viewing public can have access to a channel that will spur the growth of a burgeoning sports culture in the country. Then the entire gamut of facility, skilled organisation and informed public can come together to host, excel at and be elated by the sporting and recreational activities that are so necessary for human civilisation.

Media

Responsible Journalism is Being Heard

Tan Sri Abdullah Ahmad
Group Editor-in-Chief
The New Straits Times Press (M) Bhd

Malaysian journalism records and does manage to create a rather true-to-life mosaic of the ever-changing course of a society. It provides compelling evidence of the happenings by the irrefutable power of the written word, even in the K-economy and digital age.

It has been writ that journalists write the first draft of history. Indeed, they do as reporters of news flashes over the radio. They give voice to video clips of unfolding incidents aired intermittently over television. And their printouts provide the defining capsules of developing events, as well as lengthy speeches of politicians, including heads of state and government, that appear in daily newspapers. Reporters also record milestones in sports, business, the economy, science and in every other area of human endeavour, and increasingly these days, developments in information technology.

They also purvey details of crime, both petty and gruesome. Journals, it must be noted, came before journalists. The former are records and the latter are hacks.

Aspiring journalists acquire basic skills these days even before they assume professional careers. Mass communication and journalism courses prepare the novices rather well. In colleges and universities they learn to report and to write reports. They are taught the five Ws: what, when, where, who and why. Their teachers drill them on the importance of the inverted pyramidal structure of a news story. They are told to relate a story, as interesting as possible, in feature articles. If they can arrest the attention of the readers within the first five paragraphs, the writers can take them through the remaining thirty or forty, that is, if they can sustain the interest of their audience. Others are accepted as journalists because they have an assiduously acquired or natural felicity of language, an asset valued by editors. After recruitment, regardless of their impressive degrees, diplomas or expressive literary skills, they traditionally go through an unlearning and re-learning process. Cub reporters or cadet journalists, whatever the label, are re-trained by news, crime, business, entertainment and sports editors when raw copy is edited, sometimes with their knowledge, on occasions in their absence. Many editors want their staff to be no more than mere conduits of information.

Such an assumption is an egregious fallacy on the part of editors. For reporters, by the nature of their daily tasks, select the information or data they have gathered. Given an assignment, they attend press conferences with nothing more than brief slips of information about place, time and the person who will talk with the media.

If the news editor handing out the tasks knows his job, he will brief the reporter on what could possibly emerge in the dialogue. If the reporter is trained well, he will call for the relevant files on newspaper cuttings or surf the library online to read up on the background of the issue that would be addressed in the press conference.

But even the well-briefed and best-informed reporter attends a press conference and returns to write only his impressions. He bases his report on the press release, the dialogue he might have recorded on tape and the notes he might have jotted in his pad. And his insight. In selecting the information he presumes to be news worthy, the reporter is burdened by a weight of responsibility that might not commensurate with his age and experience.

For his raw copy, however re-crafted and shaped, might make the lead item over the 8 pm prime time television news or the next day's headlines.

But the moot question is whether reporters realise their role in the reporting and recording of unfolding events that really matter to everyone in the country. Like buying a house. Reporters of all media say that it is the right time to buy. True, interest rates are low; financing houses loudly proclaim the fact. Developers and real estates agents aver that the time is right to buy houses as prices are "moderate". Reporters echo their views. But none reports the fact that the developers are now marketing small terrace houses, 18 feet by 60 feet at RM143,000 a unit. Bigger houses, 22 feet by 72 feet are hawked at over RM257,000 each. And developers have property valued at over RM16 billion that has not been sold; that more than 50 housing projects have been abandoned. Facts all, but who relays the information to the public? Not most journalists.

One other issue touches most workers in the country, especially those reaching retirement age. The Employees Provident Fund has an Insurance Scheme, now suspended because of controversy, that allows members to parcel their savings to yield assured annual payments.

The rationale of the annuity plans is simple. You trade off your accumulated money in the Fund for assured monthly withdrawals for at least 10 years. The structure of payments is complex as actuarial principles determine the progressive disbursements. Which means the EPF member gets an increased monthly disbursement in subsequent years, more when bonuses declared by participating insurance companies, though not guaranteed but highly probable, are factored in. More importantly, the insurance scheme is optional. If members do not want to participate, they retain the right to withdraw in full all their savings at the age of 55.

The responsible journalist would have pointed out this fact in his report or the extended feature. But then, responsible journalism is difficult to define, let alone teach. Responsibility has a moral connotation. It conjures up obligations. At its simplest level, a student has the responsibility to study and study well.

A parent has the responsibility to instil in his children enduring values. A journalist has to abide by the ethics of his profession. To be fair, just and objective in all his reports and writings.

Most journalists work within these parameters. But on occasions they encounter situations where lack of information, inadequate briefs or the cultural dictates of their publishers make them select data that might or might not coalesce to present a fair and just picture of the issue they write about in their copy. That, in truth, is the albatross carried by reporters who have the moral courage to be responsible.

The journalist's job is to write and it is the editor's task to decide whether to publish. Since I became part of the *New Straits Times* in May 2000, it has been my personal responsibility to encourage reporters and writers to pen what they want as long as they are helpful, true and constructive. I have never intervened. However, whatever restraint they showed, it was of their own choosing, not imposed by their superiors, and certainly not by me.

Perhaps people should remember that editors are neither heroes nor cowards.

However, good editors train, encourage, develop and reward talent, and if they are themselves any good they ought to be able to distinguish between good and evil, no matter how each is packaged.

Foreign Perspective

of today's achievements, a new, bolder generation is accepting the challenges of the opening door. They are ready to carry on the work of the future with confidence and enthusiasm.

The American Malaysian Chamber of Commerce (AMCHAM) started in 1978. Just a few years prior, ESSO entered into production sharing agreements with Petronas, the Malaysian oil giant. About that time Andy Groves of Intel negotiated a muddy road in Penang for a possible plant site. He complained about the road to then Chief Minister, Lim Chong Eu, who made the road serviceable that same afternoon. Andy remarked, "Malaysia really gets on with things"—and the rest was history. Today, the manufacturing operations of American multinational corporations (MNCs) employ over 60,000 Malaysians and have been a mainstay of the Malaysian economy.

Texas Instruments, Motorola, Western Digital and many other electronic manufacturers followed. Technology transfer and management training were exported as American firms shared their know-how with Malaysia. IBM was established in Malaysia in 1961. It introduced the first computer system at the National Electricity Board in 1964 and the country's first online banking system in the late seventies. American hotels, franchises, banks, marketing and consulting firms and others also came on board.

AMCHAM member companies have also made substantial contributions to the communities of our host country. AMCHAM continues to coordinate the Young Enterprise Programme, with a focus on teaching students how to run companies. Science awareness kits have also been provided to teachers throughout the country.

American business has thrived in Malaysia because of a business-friendly environment, the rule of the law, orderly government processes and institutions, a solid network of infrastructure, and a hardworking, well-educated workforce. American investments in manufacturing and services have been substantial. A good measure of the conducive business environment is the billions of reinvestment dollars that pioneering investors have pumped back into the Malaysian economy over the years.

Many small and medium-sized industries (SMIs) have been spawned from American investment and technology transfer. Just as foreign direct investment and exports have been the twin engines of economic growth, entrepreneurial SMIs will be the essential drivers of continued growth in the next phase of Malaysian economic development. Building on the global network of American MNCs, many SMIs have themselves become global suppliers of products and services.

These same MNCs are leading the way into the K-economy, emerging from the brick and mortar foundation so well laid.

Over the next few years, nearly all procurement will be online and Malaysian businesses, both large and small, will realise reduced costs of operation while new global markets become more accessible. Malaysia's past successes in the global economy augurs well for continued success.

American investment and trade is now a permanent part of the Malaysian economic fabric. As Malaysia is the United States' 11th largest trading partner and the US is Malaysia's top source of foreign investment, the strategic and economic relationship continues to grow and strengthen between our two countries. The investments made include human capital as well as physical capital. Nearly 150,000 Malaysians have obtained their undergraduate and postgraduate degrees from American universities and many are now leaders of American companies here. For example, 75% of the electrical and electronics industries in Malaysia are led by Malaysians.

As research and development efforts grow, the MSC, university linkages and incubation centres help cultivate a new range of entrepreneurs. Improved educational capability and corporate linkages allow applications required by the K-economy to take hold. This will result in a new class of unique and branded Malaysian products and services to supplement and complement the directions of the new economy. Rest assured, American companies look forward to being partners in the next wave of economic growth.

Political Stability

The Pride of a Progressive Nation

Datuk Paddy Bowie
Managing Director, Paddy Schubert Sdn Bhd

The Eskimo or Innuit has 13 different words for snow, whereas in Malaysia we have only one and that we never have cause to use. The Innuit lives with snow—he builds his house with it, dresses for it, devises transport over it, no doubt shovels it away from his door every morning. It is the dominant element in his situation. He has to cope with it, manage it and therefore to define it more precisely. All businesses, all administrations are conducted within a specific milieu of social, cultural and political determinants.

The dominant element in the Malaysian situation is the multi-ethnic profile of the population which at Independence presented a unique feature—it was split exactly down the middle between the 50% indigenous bumiputras and the 50% of migrant stock. Conflict was endemic in this countervailing strength of numbers. One group held political power, the other economic power. The management of ethnic diversity is the single most compelling imperative faced by successive Governments. The outcome has been a unique Malaysian political formula to match this equally unique racial synthesis and the inescapable communal dynamics that otherwise could have torn the country apart. It has given us 44 years of peace and stability.

Malaysia has had the same Government in power in an unbroken tradition since Independence with never less than a two-thirds majority and sustained in free, fair, hard-won elections every five years. In recent years political risk—keeping scores of analysts busy overseas—is a prime consideration for business. Foreign investors need to be assured their capital and their technology are safe as well as productive. It is political stability that has underpinned the growing prosperity and sophistication of this country over the last few decades.

In recent times this has been severely tested. We are facing a leadership crisis in Asia. The first round was when the 1997 financial shock saw the exit of every political leader in the region with the exception of Singapore and Malaysia.

Dr Mahathir was the only survivor of the crisis-hit countries, as was his Government. We need to ask why.

Now we are entering a second round, ironically, in the wake of economic recovery. Again Malaysia survived, although this time more problematically.

Continued stability will depend on the strength and resilience of our political system. First, this is a mature democracy based on Westminster-style Parliamentary Elections, although the party structure is very different. There are no dictatorships, no coups d'etat—no military aspiring to political power or controlling the political estate. It is a strong, empowered Government, given the size of its majority in the House.

The dynamics of the system are its unique feature. Political parties are not so much ideologically-based as communally-oriented. The system is consensual rather than adversarial. The dominant Malay party, UMNO, commands the strategic vote and could run the country in its own right. It opts instead to share power. The Government, the National Front, is a voluntary coalition which achieves a delicate squaring off of communal interests and works on conciliation and compromise, rather in the spirit of the village 'meshuarat', where problems are thrashed through to solution, solution being consensus—win-win. There are 14 parties in the National Front Government—all the others being content to cluster around a strong UMNO and to negotiate their communal or Party interests from within rather than campaigning outside. And it works. It is UMNO's privilege as the majority Party to provide the national leadership. The Prime Minister is elected in the Party's triennial polls. Previously he was chosen by his predecessor until

Dr Mahathir opened it up to contest and democratised the system. The elected party hierarchy with an anointed Deputy ensures a smooth orderly succession. It is all very democratic.

Forty-four years in power have ensured political and policy continuity and, therefore, predictability for business. Malaysia enjoys the luxury of long-range strategic planning. The present leader can plant his flag firmly on his Vision 2020 confident even if, at 75, he may not live to see it, his Government in all likelihood will, and his plans for advanced nation status will be realised. Supporting the system is a strong institutional framework—a legacy of the British—a Judiciary and the Rule of Law based on the United Kingdom, a mature well-trained Civil Service, a sound educational system and a good working level of English, a business culture, recognisably British, conforming to the same standards of commercial practice.

The other cornerstone of the political system is a resolute leadership. This, in turn, has guaranteed social stability based on racial and religious accommodation. In a century torn apart by ethnic strife, Malaysia is a showcase of interracial harmony based on tolerance. It chooses a secular Government based on religious tolerance mandated in a multiracial, multi-sensitive society, and practices an enlightened, progressive form of Islam.

The delicate racial balance has been preserved by a series of racial contracts of which the greatest reform has been the New Economic Policy (NEP), an affirmative action programme designed to narrow the economic gap identified with race. It has been forcibly brought home of late how lucky Malaysia is to have had the NEP since this has helped to eradicate the element of economic resentment which led to problems in a neighbouring country.

Malaysia was able to get through the worst of the economic crisis protecting its people from any severe social cost. Dr. Mahathir has, in 20 years, brought a new vigour to the Government, bringing prosperity and raising the economic floor for all. Full rice bowls are the best guarantee of political and social stability. Traditionally, Malaysians have been united and disciplined and are able to live out their lives in peace and dignity.

It is a proud record.

And in the last Elections in November 1999, Malaysians, via the ballot boxes, cast their vote for more of the same. The Government was returned with the near sacred two-thirds majority, the benchmark by which we have redefined victory, since this guarantees a strong, workable Administration. Dr Mahathir himself was reaffirmed in the UMNO Elections. The Malaysian people made their choice in full accordance with Abraham Lincoln's definition of democracy.

We are now led to believe, however, that the whole system is under siege and this precious stability is at risk. The crux of the matter is that the Government, although technically entrenched at the polls, is in crisis mode, a perception confirmed when they lost the Lunas by-election. There is much to disturb. The Elections were a wake-up call, primarily in revealing the Malay community to be split. Dissent has risen and is articulated more vociferously than ever before. Malaysia bashing by the foreign media does not help. Nor does the licence of the Internet. We are confronted by the power of the press combined with the power of prejudice.

The resurgence of PAS is an alarming trend given its unchanging and non-negotiable platform for this to become a theocratic Islamic State. Malay unity upon which the Malaysian political formula is predicated is now threatened and the contest is joined as to who should represent the majority Malay vote. The endgame is succession.

If the ugly face of politics appears in power play or in fighting within, we can forget our hard-won stability.

Dr Mahathir declared in his New Year message two aspirations for 2001—to re-unite the Malays and reinstate racial harmony. It will be necessary to reach out to the presently disaffected youth, to close the deepening gap between the grassroots and the leadership and to tackle the issues that have become the lightning rod of dissent. It is the year of the Snake. The political snake may have to shed its skin and reinvent itself to meet the exigencies of the time, i.e. a national reconstruction.

But one thing is for sure. If we are to defend our proud record of political stability we need unity, not divisiveness. And whilst just demands must be heard and met, it is very easy to take to the streets and call for *Reformasi*. Demonstrations are not the way. To destroy is easier than to construct. We need *Transformasi* rather than *Reformasi* (but will subsume the latter). What we need is a concrete agenda for change and reform. Calling for political will, strategic thinking and above all, resolute leadership. Malaysia is no stranger to these attributes. They have given us in the past the political stability we took for granted. It is a tried and tested formula.

INDEX

OTHER TITLES ON MALAYSIA
published by Asean Academic Press

ECONOMIC CRISES IN MALAYSIA
CAUSES, IMPLICATIONS AND POLICY PRESCRIPTIONS
Samuel Bassey Okposin & Cheng Ming Yu

This study identifies the various economic crises that has plagued Malaysia since 1957. Besides examining theoretical debates and causes of each of these crises, it also discusses the economic impact of each of these crises in relation to the economy and looks at the policy measure adopted for each crisis. This is the first time that all crises since Malaysia's independence have been documented in a single volume.

Five major crises have been identified between 1956 and 1999, namely the early commodity crisis of 1956-72, the first oil crisis of 1973-74, the second commodity/oil crisis of 1980-81, the electronic/third commodity crisis of 1985-86, and the Asian currency crisis of 1997-98. Although the latter has received much attention from the media, academia and observers, this study not only looks at this crisis but also the ones before, how they have evolved over the years and the relationship between them.

Samuel Bassey Okposin is a Senior Lecturer at the Faculty of Management, Multimedia University, Malaysia. *Cheng Ming Yu* is a lecturer at the Faculty of Management of the same university.

208pp ISBN 1 901919 32 3 £45.00

MULTIMEDIA SUPER CORRIDOR: A JOURNEY TO EXCELLENCE IN INSTITUTIONS OF HIGHER LEARNING
Norsaidatul Akmar Mazelan, Martin Harnevie & Aberlado C. Valida

This book, besides providing vital information for IHLs, especially those involved in granting multimedia or IT-specific qualifications, rationalises the need to thrive for excellence to meet the needs of modern industry. Constant changes in processes, technology and markets mean that government and industry will expect IHLs to meet their demand for skilled knowledge workers. This is in consonance with job-growth projections in the services sector, including transportation, communication, finance, insurance, real estate, and the wholesale and retail trade. As such, governments must enhance efforts at developing an effective workforce that is equipped with the latest technological capabilities.

Norsaidatul Akmar Mazelan is the Senior Manager of Corporate Planning and Head of the Executive Chairman Office at the Multimedia Development Corporation, Malaysia. *Martin Harnevie* is the Managing Director of Money Vector, a Malaysian-based company specialising in Strategic Management, Knowledge Management and Market Intelligence for the multimedia industry. *Aberlado C. Valida* is the Manager of the Higher Education Client Service Unit at the Multimedia Development Corporation, Malaysia.

192pp ISBN 1 901919 14 5 £45.00

CULTURAL CONTESTATIONS: MEDIATING IDENTITIES IN A CHANGING MALAYSIAN SOCIETY

Edited by Zawawi Ibrahim

Forty-two years after Malaysia's independence, can we safely outline a Malaysian identity? Has an emerging middle class affected social transformation in the various states? How do the Chinese view Malay hegemony in the peninsula? This book combines fresh and critical perspectives in the analysis of the Malaysian nation-state and its postcolonial social transformation. It investigates development as a process of cultural contestation in which new social meanings or identities are continuously being constituted, renegotiated and reconstructed, involving the state, institutions, classes and other groups of social actors. It recognises mediating identities as a crucial process in the whole phenomenon of the emergence, consolidation and sustainability of the modern nation-state.

Zawawi Ibrahim, a social anthropologist, is professor of sociology and dean of the Faculty of Applied and Creative Arts at Universiti Malaysia Sarawak, Malaysia.

Published in association with the center for Southeast Asian Studies, Kyoto University, Tokyo, Japan

212pp ISBN 1 901919 04 8 £45.00

THE CHANGING PHASES OF MALAYSIAN ECONOMY

Samuel Bassey Okposin, Abdul Halim Abdul Hamid & Ong Hway Boon

This book examines the changing phases of the Malaysian economy since independence in 1957. Agriculture was the main source of growth in the 1950s; in the 1960s and 1970s, import-substitution and export-oriented industrialisation propelled economic growth. In the 1980s, investment and the growing service sector was the engine of growth. In the 1990s, the economy is sustained through productivity and industrial upgrading to higher value-added industries. Besides addressing the various cyclical downturns and as the speculative attack on Asian economies, this book also deals with issues pertaining to agricultural transformation, tourism development, privatisation, environmental and manpower development. The arduous tasks involved in attaining the achievements of the last four decades were brought to a virtual standstill in mid-1997 due to the Asian financial crisis. However, the Malaysian economy has benefited much from the government's policy of selective capital controls, despite opposition. Besides breaking the vicious downward spiral that the exchange rate instability had set in motion, capital control measures were also used to minimise the negative impact of large short-term capital inflows and outflows.

Samuel Bassey Okposin is a Senior Lecturer at the Faculty of Management, Universiti Multimedia, Malaysia. *Abdul Halim Abdul Hamid* is the Coordinator of the Finance Group at the Faculty of Management. *Ong Hway Boon* is working on a project in relation to the role of multimedia economics in Malaysia.

312pp ISBN 1 901919 25 0 £45

THE TRANSFORMATION OF AN IMMIGRANT SOCIETY: A STUDY OF THE CHINESE IN SABAH

Danny Wong Tze-ken

This is a story about the Chinese living in the East Malaysian state of Sabah on the island of Borneo, a people representing part of the wider spectrum of the population outside mainland China. It is the history of the Chinese who had braved the odds and ventured to build their livelihood in a foreign land before and during World War II from 1881 to 1946. Sharing a common root, the Chinese of Sabah and their other Southeast Asian counterparts possess many similarities, yet within these similarities are variants which distinguish them from the rest. Apart from being the largest non-indigenous ethnic group in Sabah, they also stand out in many ways in relation to the other Chinese communities in Malaysia. Distinctively prevalent among the Chinese of Sabah is its large composition of Hakkas, thus making the Hakka dialect the lingua franca of the Chinese in the state, a feature few can parallel in Malaysia or Southeast Asia. Within this community is a large number of Christians, forming some 30 per cent of the total Chinese population in Sabah. The Chinese of Sabah also stamped their prominence when they staged an open uprising against the Japanese Army during World War II, despite a dearth of resources and manpower, a feat few communities in Southeast Asian could equal or emulate. Even in local politics, they have proved to be different as they build themselves into a cohesive political force, and have to this day provided the state with two chief ministers. This books provides a backdrop to these dominant features and an insight into what made the Chinese of Sabah who they are today.

Danny Wong Tze-ken is a lecturer in the Department of History at the University of Malaya in Kuala Lumpur, Malaysia.

238pp ISBN 1 901919 16 1 £45

MALAYSIA TODAY TOWARDS THE NEW MILLENNIUM: A COLLECTION OF ESSAYS ON VARIOUS ASPECTS OF MALAYSIA'S ECONOMY

Asian Strategy and Leadership Institute

This book chronicles Malaysia's achievements and provides an insight into the nation today and its future direction. By delving into areas as diverse as economics, infrastructure, industry, defence and foreign policy, and the Malaysian experience, it paints a picture of farsighted strategic thinking and planning, determined leadership and the search for solutions to age-old problems. To remain globally competitive, Malaysia will have to depend on its ability to promote new sources of growth. Capital-intensive and high value-added technology-based industries will be the cornerstone of its economic development strategy.

Published in association with the Asian Strategy and Leadership Institute (ASLI) in Kuala Lumpur, Malaysia

352pp ISBN 1 901919 03 X £45.00

THE SINDHIS OF MALAYSIA

Maya Khemlani David

This sociolinguistic study of the Sindhi-Hindu community in Malaysia investigates language maintenance and shift of this group. The Sindhis are an urban, ethnolinguistic minority comprising less than a thousand people in multilingual Malaysia. The author provides a detailed ethnography of communication in Sindhi homes in Malaysia. She focuses on generational changes in language choice preferences and code switching strategies.

This study offers a substantial amount of systematically collected empirical data. Language choice in the home, intra-community interactions and in the public domain is investigated. The Sindhi community has shifted from Sindhi to an international language, English and, to some extent, Malay. However, the Sindhi language still has some functional uses and Sindhi words are retained in mixed English-Malay speech. This shift reflects the utilitarian and pragmatic attitude of this upwardly-mobile community.

Maya Khemlani David is an associate professor at the Faculty of Languages and Linguistics in the University of Malaya, Kuala Lumpur Malaysia. Dr David's research interest is in sociolinguistics with a special focus on the maintenance and shift of the languages of minority communities in Malaysia. She has researched language choices of both the Portuguese community in Malacca and the Tamil community in Kuala Lumpur. She is currently working on the language choices of the Punjabi-Sikh community in the Klang Valley.

232pp ISBN 1 901919 13 7 £45.00

DISABLED PEOPLE: CITIZENSHIP AND SOCIAL WORK: THE MALAYSIAN EXPERIENCE

Denison Jayasooria

What place do disabled people have in Malaysian society? Will they remain marginalised and ignored or can they become independent and self-reliant citizens? Many disabled people are merely recipients of handouts and charity. But with opportunity and chance, they can have dignity and a sense of self-worth.

These questions and issues form part of this interesting study by scholar-activist Denison Jayasooria, who also looks at wider concerns of citizenship rights, justice, equal opportunity, social work models and practices and national welfare policies.

This is a major and rare piece of work on disability issues, disabled people, policies and also the future direction of this significant segment of society. It will help readers gain a better understanding of the struggles of disabled people in their quest for a meaningful and productive life in a nation heading towards industrialised-nation status.

324pp ISBN1 901919 18 8 £50.00

DEFENDING MALAYSIA: FACING THE 21ST CENTURY

Mohamad Najib Abdul Razak

The end to the cold war was both abrupt and dramatic. Since then, the world has been in a state of flux. In Asia, old wounds that were once put aside are now finding expression in various forms. From great power rivalries to territorial disputes, regional countries are now being confronted with grave challenges. This is being compounded by domestic instability that appears to rear its ugly head. Nation-states are being threatened in many parts of the world.

Malaysia has been able to sustain political and economic stability, achieving growth and prosperity. This is being achieved through prudent policies predicted on the creation of an equitable society. This is Malaysia's guiding philosophy.

Malaysia has also managed its security environment well, continuing to face the emerging challenges of the 21st century. Based on a collection of selected speeches, this book covers both domestic and international issues that have ramifications on policy formulation.

Mohamad Najib Abdul Razak is the Malaysian Minister of Defence. He has held a number of other ministerial appointments, including Minister of Youth and Sports, Minister of Education and the Chief Minister of the State of Pahang. He has been in politics for over 25 years and is currently vice-president of UMNO, the ruling party since independence. He was previously the head of UMNO Youth.

104 pp ISBN 1 901919 36 6 £29.00